RIDING THE WHITE HORSE

AND LIVING IN ITS SHADOW

Riding the white horse is an analogy

used for experiencing heroin.

By David Michael Straw

© Copyright 2018 David Michael Straw

All rights reserved.

No part of this publication may be reproduced, stored in a retrieval system, or transmitted, in any form or by any means, electronic, mechanical, photocopying, recording or otherwise, without the prior written permission of the publisher.

British Library Cataloguing in Publication Data.

A catalogue record for this book is available from the British Library

ISBN 978 0 86071 774 4

ACKNOWLEDGEMENTS

I would like to thank all those who have supported and assisted me in any way with the writing of this book, and the journey I have travelled since Gary's death. In particular I would like to mention the following people who provided their help in so many different ways. I have listed them in no particular order so as not to prioritise anyone.

Debbie Knowles her daughter and all the team at Hetty's Charity for typing, Angela Rigley of Eastwood Writers Group for editing, Chad Critchley, my good friend, for his support and the foreword. Mick Taylor my long standing school friend, the Eastwood Baptist Church, and of course my wife Elizabeth, for their help and support.

RIDE THE WHITE HORSE

'Ride the white horse', isn't that what they say?

But to sit in the saddle, a price you must pay.

At first, I will amaze you, you will dream of my power,

I will be there to seduce you, no matter the hour.

I will comfort you and hold you so safe in my arms,

You will wonder, from where do I get my subliminal charms.

You will tingle and tremble at the thrill that I give,

And without me, you will feel your life you can't live.

Before too long your love will turn slowly to hate.

You won't be able to leave me, your need will be great.

You will try to desert me; I will drive you insane;

Not content to inhale me, you will drive me deep in your vein.

Your life will be ruined; it all turns to dust,

You know you can't leave me, but you feel that you must.

To cheat and to steal, there won't be a care.

Just so long as I am near, I have to be there.

I will start to destroy you; it goes on till the end.

You will try to forsake me but your ways you can't mend.

You desire me, you want me, I am all that you crave,

I will always be with you as you go to your grave.

David Michael Straw 2016

Riding the White Horse is an analogy used for

the taking of the illegal drug heroin

Dedication

I dedicate this book to my late son, Gary, so much loved and so sadly missed.

Gary David Straw

1st September 1975 - 18th January 2016

I loved the boy with the utmost love

Of which my soul is capable

And he is taken from me.

Yet in the agony of my spirit,

In surrendering such treasure, I feel a thousand times richer

Than if I had never possessed it.

I have written this book with true sincerity and honesty, for without that there would be no point in writing it in the first place. None of the facts mentioned are meant to be harmful or malicious, and to anyone who may be in any way offended, I apologise in advance.

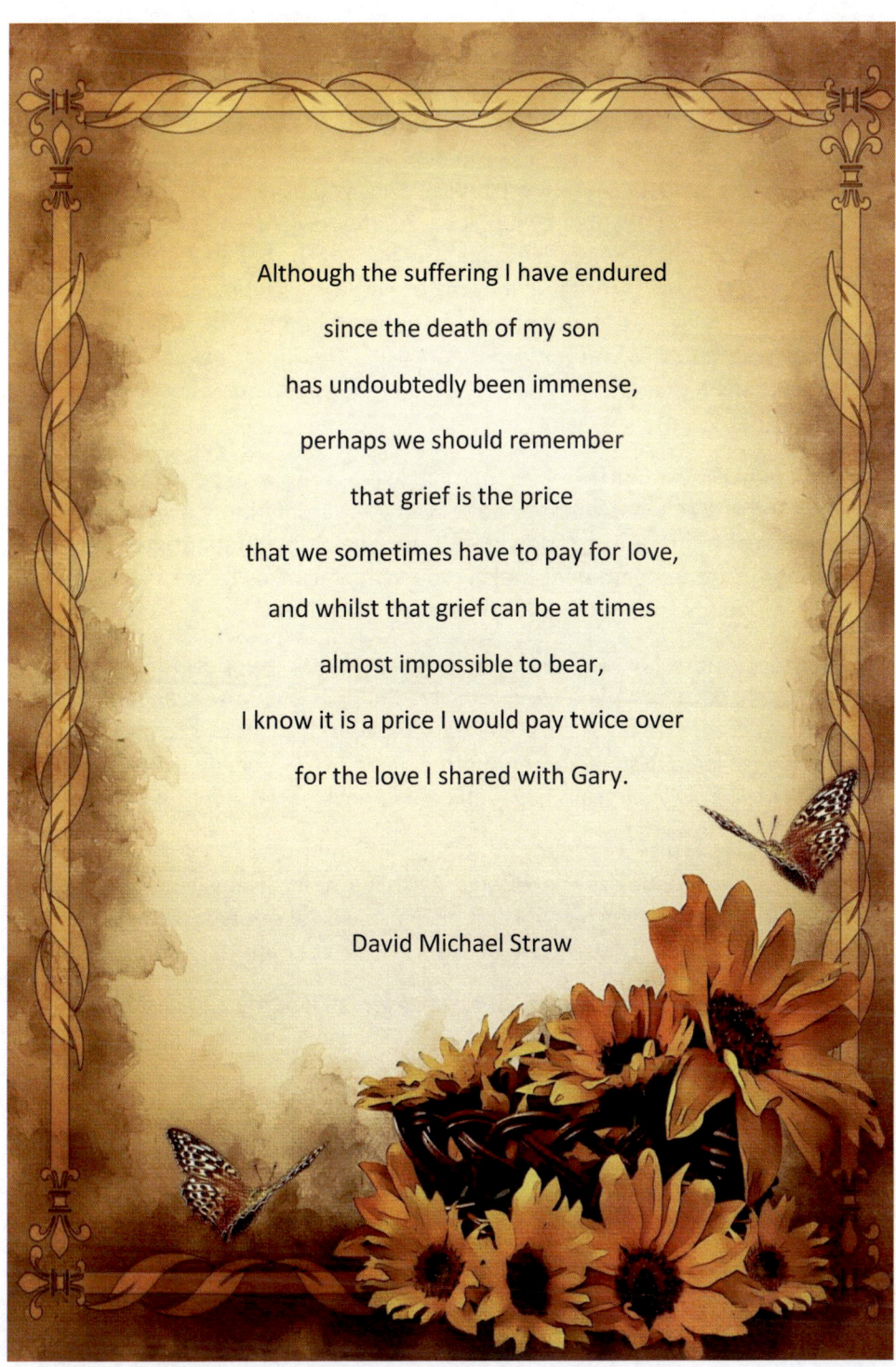

Although the suffering I have endured

since the death of my son

has undoubtedly been immense,

perhaps we should remember

that grief is the price

that we sometimes have to pay for love,

and whilst that grief can be at times

almost impossible to bear,

I know it is a price I would pay twice over

for the love I shared with Gary.

David Michael Straw

PREFACE

For some of you who pick up this book and casually flip through the pages, it may mean nothing, and you may put it aside and think no more of it. That is good, because it probably means you have not suffered the traumatic loss of someone you love to the evil of drugs. For the thousands of others whose lives, and the lives of those loved ones who have been affected by drugs, it may mean a little more; it may even bring a tear to your eye. That was not the intention when I wrote my story. I simply wanted to record my experiences and the life of my son, Gary, and perhaps to warn others and give them an insight into what is often a world of pain and anguish.

It may invoke memories of events you have already experienced, or enlighten you to what you may have yet to endure. Either way, if it can convey just a little of the knowledge I have gained with hindsight and, perhaps just one person not making the same mistakes I have made, it will have been worth writing for that reason alone.

This story is not a fairy tale, it doesn't begin with "Once upon a time" and it certainly doesn't have a "And they lived happily ever after" ending. It is instead a true reflection of a life marred by drugs, of how it really is or at the very least, how it can be. But how can I truly convey to you the pain and sorrow that drugs have inflicted upon my life?

I cannot play you any haunting or atmospheric music, I cannot show you the latest and exciting special effects. All I have at my disposal are words. Now words, if used correctly, can be very powerful but whether I have the necessary skills to use them in this way I don't know.

Whether I can give you an insight however small into my world of pain I have no idea.

The only way to discover the answer to this is to read my story and then it is for you to decide if I have even come anywhere close to achieving my goal.

FOREWORD by Chad Critchley

In 1996 I was spending a few days fishing on Moorgreen Reservoir, Nottinghamshire. On the opposite side to where I was fishing, I saw a man pushing what looked like a swan on a wheelbarrow. He quickly disappeared behind the trees. I saw the same a week later, and then on the third occasion, he was on the same side of the reservoir that I was fishing. The swan on a wheelbarrow turned out to be a wheelbarrow containing fishing and camping equipment with a white duvet on top, covering it all! Pushing this was a tall, grey-haired man who introduced himself to me as Dave. We spent the next couple of days fishing next to each other and struck up a friendship that has lasted since that time.

We continued to fish together for a number of years and during this time I learned that Dave had a son who I actually knew, called Gary. I attended the same schools as Gary from a young age, and although I never mixed in the same circles as Gary at school, we crossed paths on a regular basis and we were always friendly with each other. Without going in to detail, I was aware that Gary tended to mix with people at school who were known to be the ones that skipped lessons, the ones that smoked and the ones that got in to trouble on a regular basis. I had a different group of friends so didn't get mixed up in any of that. Regardless of this, Gary was always friendly with me whenever I saw him.

As the school years ended and everyone went their separate ways with work or further education, I moved away with the army, and upon leaving the forces, I lived in an area that meant I never crossed paths with anyone from school. It was at this time that I started fishing Moorgreen Reservoir and met Dave.

Dave and I had many conversations while relaxing on the bankside, as time was of no issue. Among these conversations Dave confided in me on the issues he was now having with Gary in relation to getting into trouble and starting to abuse drugs. At this time the issues were intermittent and Gary would be on them one week and off them the next. However I always had a sense that Dave was never telling me everything, and that the issues were maybe worse than he was letting on. Dave had bought up Gary as a single parent, and as a result they had a father and son bond that was very strong, so I can wholly understand that pride would prevent him telling me every detail.

During the years we fished at Moorgreen Reservoir Gary had a spell where he tried to take himself away from the people he was mixing with, and get away from the drugs. This appeared to be working and as a result Dave set him up in work and with a vehicle, and Gary seemed to be sticking with this and working hard. During this time Gary bought himself some fishing tackle and started coming fishing with Dave and me, and when I wasn't there it was Father and son, and they became fishing partners! On the many occasions he came with us, I never saw a side of him that would suggest he abused drugs, or that he had a side to him that was not pleasant. He was sociable, funny, polite and helpful and it did look as though he was turning a corner in his life.

It was around this time that I started fishing further afield in Hertfordshire so the time Dave and I fished together was limited, but we still ensured we had the odd day's fishing, or met up for a cuppa to catch up. I also had a massive change in career and became a Police Officer, and I think it was partly because of this change in career that Dave began to confide in me more on the subject of drugs, my experience of dealing with them and the effects on people involved in them. It was clear to me from what Dave was asking and speaking about on the occasions we met that Gary had gone downhill and was now beginning to struggle with drugs, and that it was having a major impact on Gary, Dave and both of their lives. I will not delve any further on the details, as this book will give you the insight in to their lives and the impact drug abuse had.

What I will mention is my experience of dealing with persons in my career so far who abuse drugs. I have seen people from a young age start with smoking, move on to cannabis and progress on to harder drugs such as cocaine and heroin, not to mention all of the synthetic drugs available now. The reasons for persons going down this road can differ massively. It could be one or a combination of many, such as some form of trauma in their life, family background, mixing with the wrong crowd or simply having an addictive personality. None of the reasons necessarily mean the individual is a bad person, but when under the influence of drugs and desperate for the next hit, they become someone else, their boundaries and morals change, the drugs rule them. I have only ever known one addict, who was addicted to Heroin, get clean. Whether he still is now or not I do not know, but in 15 years of service, only having seen one, shows how difficult it can be.

Gary was not a bad person, in fact quite the contrary, the true Gary was friendly, sociable, polite, hardworking and clever, but when the drugs took hold he changed, and over the years the drugs slowly took over, to the point where he gave everything to them.

What follows is a heart-rending story of the battles that father, son and drugs had. To me it is a remarkable story, and one that shows how strong a father and son bond can be and the lengths a father will go to when he sees his son struggling. I experienced some of it over the years through knowing both Dave and Gary, but this book goes into details that not even I knew.

GARY AND DRUGS AN INTRODUCTION

When I had finished writing my story, upon reading through it afterwards, I realised that other than details contained in certain passages, I had not given a description of my son as a person. I realised this was not an error that I could leave uncorrected, and so I will begin to attempt to give an impression of the real Gary.

Someone who I believe I knew better than he knew himself and someone who I loved unconditionally.

Gary as a child and an adult was always a gentle person, he might not have thanked me for that description because it was not an image he had of himself. He always liked to be thought of as one of the boys a bit of a lad but in truth despite the image he tried to portray of himself even when he reached adulthood, despite his age and physical size, he possessed a childlike quality, one of naivety and innocence. I do not say that in a derogative way, far from it in fact because this quality was one I found endearing.

My own school reports very often would contain the words "is easily led" and this was only too true of Gary. He needed to be accepted as one of the gang and if it meant doing things that were contrary to his nature then so be it.

On one occasion as a teenager Gary and a group of his friends had been in trouble with the police for stealing a postman's mail trolley that had been left at the top of a drive, as the postman had delivered the letters to that address. Gary and his friends had seen the mail trolley as they drove past in a car. Gary was the one who had jumped out of the car and actually taken the mail and placed it in the car. I was not there to witness the incident but in my mind's eye I can imagine Gary exclaiming 'I will do it, I will go and get it'. I am not proclaiming Gary as an innocent, because he wasn't but it would have been a typical act to prove himself as a top man, as one of the boys. This trait had been with Gary all through his childhood and remained with him until his sad demise.

The true Gary was a kind and gentle person who would help anyone and he would share whatever he owned selflessly, but he felt he always had to prove his worth. He hadn't got a malicious bone in his body and despite an image he tried to portray, the gang culture was not really his scene, in reality he was an interloper.

When I speak of Gary involved with gangs I do not mean he was involved in the gang culture of violence that we so often witness today. In fact, describing Gary and his friends as a gang is a stretch of the imagination anyway, they were just drug addicts who found each other.

Gary was never violent; he never carried a weapon like so many people do today. Yes, he got himself into trouble with the police for minor shoplifting, and whilst I obviously do not condone this act, Gary never participated in mugging anyone, or burglary or any other serious crime. Any criminal act was alien to Gary's nature and I do not try to infer Gary was some sort of saint because he wasn't, but I stress once more, and will do so again the power these drugs exert over people and how it changes them has to be seen to be believed.

Gary had a love of nature and a fascination with it, he was never cruel and loved and cherished all animals. On many occasions as a bird sang its melody from whatever perch it sat upon he would mimic its songs so perfectly it would reply and so it would continue until one or the other of them ceased their whistling.

As a child he had so many different interests and always wanted to be a part of whatever was happening. He was always on the go, so full of energy, none of that changed as he grew older. Gary was never afraid of hard work or getting his hands dirty. Gary was not an academic, but he was intelligent although his decision making was somewhat flawed.

He always wanted to impress, his first car was a Ford Cosworth, not a wise choice considering his age and finances, but in his eyes it made him out to be someone of importance, someone to look up to amongst his friends and something that ended up as a disaster.

I can only imagine when he first started to participate in the drug scene that it was a similar scenario.

With hindsight I now realize that drugs were everywhere, they were a part of the social scene, and again Gary would have become involved not least of all because he would have felt that taking them would have made him look cool, made him a part of the action.

The drugs of course ultimately changed Gary as they invariably do with anyone who becomes a drug addict. On the surface he became selfish, self-obsessed to the exclusion of anyone else and at times unpleasant to be with. He alternated from the Gary of old to the new selfish person he could be, but underneath the real Gary was still there, he still surfaced and gave you hope, and that is why it was so agonising so utterly destroying.

Gary tried to break free from the drugs so many times and for long periods he succeeded, but ultimately their power was too strong and he always fell under their influence once again. In the latter years of his drug abuse he did gain some control and he behaved more like the person he really was. The lies and deceit, the stealing from his family to fund his habit subsided, he was more responsible, but never the less they still controlled his life.

I always hoped Gary would find himself a steady girlfriend and establish a long term relationship. I felt that if anything, that could be the one thing that altered his path in life. Unfortunately it never happened,, why I don't know?, he was a good looking lad, although obviously his drug habit was not a good trait, other drug users seem to find a partner in life, but for Gary it never happened. He had a few short term relationships but nothing ever developed and I can't help but wonder if he had found that special one, could it have saved him?, but of course now we will never know.

Many people have a strong revulsion of anyone who uses drugs in this way and it is an attitude I can so easily understand. So many drug addicts and drug dealers are evil people, but some of them like Gary are the casualties of life. When you see a drug addict and form an opinion based on what you see be careful because the outward appearance can be deceptive. Underneath can be the real personality, a person not evil but someone who has become a victim themselves, a victim of the scourge of drugs, someone carried along on an unstoppable tide of misery and desperation. Someone who is kind, loving and gentle, someone like my son Gary who began his descent into what became a world of underlying misery.

You could argue that Gary could have halted that descent and climbed his way back to the top, but believe me when I tell you he did try, he tried so very hard, but the road was for Gary too steep. He gained a foothold on so many occasions, but it always crumbled beneath him, and he failed to climb back into the sunlight, he descended so far that there was no return, no redemption and he paid the ultimate price, just like so many people before him and like so many more who will follow him

They pay that price not for being wicked or evil, but for lacking that inner strength to break free of what is such a malignant force. It is a force so strong that the majority of us lack an understanding of its power to utterly and completely take over someone's life, and ultimately destroy it.

Had I not witnessed it for myself I would not have believed it possible. I would have stood there and stated that if my son or daughter had become involved in taking drugs I would have taken control, made sure they became clean, given them all the help and understanding to ensure they became free of drugs.

I tried to do my best for Gary but I still failed him, could I have done more? Yes I could, and I must carry that thought with me for the rest of my days. But in my defence I lacked the knowledge, patience and understanding to make the right decisions.

Faced with the same situation again I still don't know what is the right course of action other than to be there for them if and when they need you. I involved the experts and I did what I thought was right but it ultimately failed and all I can say to someone whose children or grandchildren become involved in the misuse of drugs, is be afraid, be very afraid because it is so powerful, so malignant that very few people can take back control of their lives.

When I first felt the need to write this book, it was in the early days after my son's death, but as I did so I realised I had started part way through my story and so I will now begin at the beginning.

CHAPTER 1

I had gone to bed on the night of August 31st 1975. My wife was carrying our twins but there were complications: one or both of them was impatient to see the outside world, but the trouble was it was seven weeks too early, so she went into Derby City Hospital for monitoring, and to try to delay the birth.

I was awakened in the early hours of the following morning by the ringing of the telephone in the hall. I tumbled out of bed, still half asleep, and half ran and half fell downstairs to answer it. The voice on the other end confirmed my identity and then told me my wife had given birth to twin boys. Unfortunately, because they were premature, things were not so good and with the second-born things were very serious, and could I get there as soon as possible. I quickly threw on my clothes and jumped into the car and raced through the darkness at high speed. I told myself if I get stopped for speeding surely the police would understand; looking back, I doubt they would have.

I arrived at the hospital and raced to the maternity ward. I was told my wife was doing well but both boys were fighting for their lives. The first-born was given the better chance but with the second-born his brain had been starved of oxygen due to the cord being wrapped around his neck and, even if he had lived, he would more than probably be brain damaged. I thanked the doctor for his honesty and he took me to see my wife.

We were both obviously devastated by the news and as we looked at the two incubators, watching those tiny and helpless human beings, both of which only weighed three pounds, we prayed that against all the odds, they would survive. What should have been our happiest and proudest moment was in fact our very worst.

We were advised soon after to name our second-born child and he would be quickly baptised.

Before we knew we were having twins we had decided, if it was a boy, we would call him Michael, so that is what we named our second-born son.

Michael survived for what was, for us all, nearly two agonising days but, eventually, he lost his fight for life and passed away. Despite the warnings we had been given it was devastating, but we consoled ourselves by saying if he had been brain damaged it was perhaps a blessing. Even so, we were distraught.

We then turned all our prayers and hopes to our first-born and although he gave us many scares, he gradually grew stronger and began to gain weight. After six weeks in the hospital, upon reaching a weight of six pounds, we were allowed to take him home, providing we kept him warm. We left the central heating on day and night. It was a worrying time but as it turned out, he was fit and strong and grew into a healthy baby and toddler. After what we had been through, he was very precious and we christened him Gary David.

It would be nice to continue this story by saying all was well and he had a normal happy childhood, but my wife had previously been diagnosed with acute schizophrenia and whilst I will not go into details, our life became a nightmare.

My wife eventually filed for divorce due to my unreasonable behaviour. You have to understand there was no unreasonable behaviour! It was all down to my wife's illness, but to her it was all very real.

I always stood by my wife through her years of illness but, eventually, I realised it was out of control, and after years of distress I couldn't carry on living a nightmare, and our marriage was over.

My wife went to live with her mother and I was left to look after Gary as a single parent. Because it was many months later when the custody case went to court and also because of my wife's illness, I was granted full time custody. Gary was five years old at the time.

I never once bad mouthed my wife to Gary and I always encouraged him to see her. What had happened between us had nothing to do with Gary's relationship with his mum. At one point she wanted a reconciliation, but I knew it was just a brief interlude in her illness. There had been many over the years and I knew nothing had changed. I couldn't go back to living my life the way I had.

I always tried to be there for her if I could; it was not her fault she was ill, but I could not go back. Obviously, as much as possible, Gary was shielded from any fallout, but it must have influenced his early years.

Before our final breakup we had all moved to our new home, a bungalow I had built for my family to live in. When my wife left me to bring up Gary alone, I initially needed time off work. When I explained my situation to my employer at that time, I won't say he wasn't understanding, but he finished me there and then. He even told the D.H.S.S it was me who quit my job and it was weeks before I received any money for being unemployed. In addition to this, I obviously had to give my wife a monetary settlement so I had to take out a mortgage on the bungalow and pay my wife her share.

It was almost a year before I returned to full time employment, and money was always tight, but that year I spent with Gary was one of the happiest of my life. Some of the memories from that time, although seemingly trivial, remain etched in our minds.

Gary would return home from school for his lunch, which I prepared and, whilst we ate our lunch, we would watch the television for a short while; there would be around thirty minutes of children's programmes at that time. One of Gary's favourites was a programme called Button Moon and right up until the time of Gary's death, if ever the topic was raised, we would look at each other and both say together, 'Button Moon, come back soon'. Words that ended the programme, and words that we both remembered with much fondness.

Another memory of his early years was another silly one, but it became a nightly routine when he was very young. When I put him in bed, I would always say to him before I left the room, 'Nighty, nighty' and he would reply, 'Pyjama, pyjama'. As I said, it was just silliness but it stuck with us for a number of years.

One night, shortly before his death, he texted me to say, *See you tomorrow. I am going to bed.* For no reason, the memory of those early years came into my head and I wondered if Gary still remembered. I texted him the words, *Nighty Nighty* and sure enough he did; back came the words, *Pyjama pyjama.* Such silly little episodes and there were so many others, but all the same they reinforced our bond with each other; we were so close, so in tune with each other. It was so wonderful whilst he was alive but so painful to remember after his death.

Although I was a single parent, I cannot take all the credit for looking after Gary on my own. My mum and aunt helped me tremendously and I have no idea how I would have managed without them.

Unfortunately, for Gary there was no Grandfather on my side of the family to have a relationship with. My own mum had brought me up as a single parent herself, and when I was born in 1950 that would have been quite a stigma, both for my mum and her parents and for myself. Other children can be so very cruel and many times I was taunted because I had no father. I will leave it to your imagination to guess what they taunted me with. I never knew my father and to this day, I know nothing about him; my mum refused to tell me any information right up until the day she died in October 2000.

I guess my father is also dead by this time and I don't suppose I will ever know who he was, My aunt did give me a photograph of him when he was a young man, after my mum's death, and all my aunt would tell me was that it wasn't to be for him and my mum.

I don't know if he knew I even existed. Although I never had a father, I always felt I had two mothers. My mum's sister who never married and had no children of her own played a huge part in my life until her death in August 2015, just a few months before I was too lose Gary.

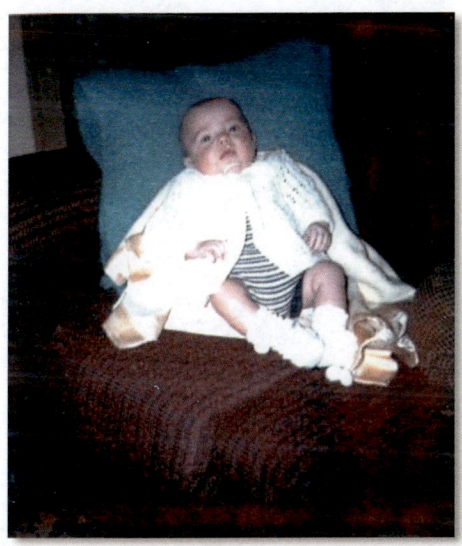

Gary David as a baby

Gary with Grandma Jessie

Gary with Great Aunt Kath

Gary feeding ducks

Day out at Shipley Park

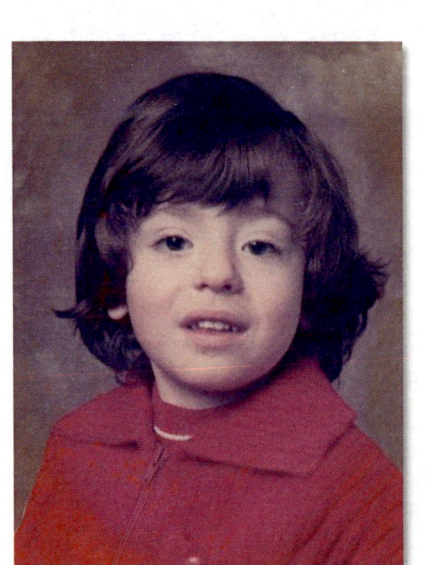

Early school photograph

CHAPTER 2

Gary was enrolled at the local infant school and he continued to do well, although his progress was perhaps a little slower than most of the other children in his age group. He had even been slower in learning to walk and even talk, but I was told that this was quite normal for someone who had been born prematurely.

Gary was a popular child and he had many friends; it wasn't very often one or several of them wouldn't be running around in our house. If Gary and I went anywhere together the usual cry was, 'Can I take my friends?'

You wouldn't be allowed to do it these days but the back of the van would often be filled with his friends. When we arrived at our destination Gary would be in front with them and I would wander after them all on my own. I didn't mind, in fact I was delighted; it was wonderful to watch them enjoying themselves.

Gary still continued to see his mum but, to be honest, sometimes it was a little bit upsetting because, instead of spending several days at his mum's house, he wanted to stay at home and be with all of his friends. I always encouraged him to go, and stressed the importance to him of spending time with his mum.

Looking back, I realised I spoilt him but he was so very special to me and I loved him so much. It's no excuse, I know, but there we are. We had so many holidays and adventures together and my whole life revolved around Gary. Perhaps too much, with hindsight.

Gary had so many interests. We went camping and fishing, he joined a local football club and later on, a boxing club as well, plus he still had many friends and was always busy doing something or other. He spent a lot of time with his grandmother and great aunt who I know spoilt him as well.

On his birthdays, the 1st September, we would go to the American Adventure at Shipley Park. It always seemed to coincide with a really hot sunny day and I would take Gary and a van load of his friends there. I would pay the entrance fee for all of us and, once inside, all of the rides and entertainments were free. They used to really enjoy themselves and I have some wonderful memories of these happy days.

As I said earlier, I had begun full time work after a year off and I had started working for a friend at my trade as a plumber and heating engineer. After a few years, although I still continued to do his work for him, I went self-employed which gave me more flexibility with the hours I worked.

Gary continued his schooling and as time passed he progressed to junior school. He continued to do well and he was obviously quite intelligent. Where he got that from remains a mystery.

He had a fairly normal life, apart from not having a full time mum, and whatever my shortcomings as a father, I know he had a full and very happy childhood.

He wasn't a sickly child but I remember one night he developed croup and I rushed him to hospital in a panic, because he was constantly coughing and barking like a seal. I didn't know at the time what it was, but it turned out not to be serious. I had to continuously boil a kettle in his room for the rest of the night to help him breathe. None of the doors would shut for a week because of the damp.

On another occasion he had a series of minor injuries. He hurt his leg quite badly playing football; it was so bad he needed physio for quite a long time. Then he fell off his bike and again had to go to hospital, and he also ran over his own fingers with his skateboard whilst riding on it. The nurses at Ilkeston hospital nicknamed him Buster.

Gary eventually went to the comprehensive school and things continued to go well. Gary was growing up fast and they were happy days.

When Gary was around the age of twelve things changed a little.

I had met a lady called, Elizabeth. As things developed we became close and after around two years we married and we all lived together in our original family home. I ensured my time with Gary was not compromised and we all had some great times together.

Gary did not seem in the least put out and in fact seemed to embrace the situation; thankfully they got on really well together. In fact I asked Gary to be my best man. He was only fourteen years old and we didn't ask him to make a speech but, apart from that, he carried out the rest of his duties really well and he seemed only too pleased to have been asked. Everyone was really proud of him.

His stepmum, though, was a little stricter with him than I had been, and his days of him being spoilt at home were over, although I suspect his grandmother and great aunt continued to spoil him as usual.

It was around this time when Gary decided he wanted more than just pocket money and he asked me if he could get himself a paper round. I wasn't overly keen for I didn't want him going out before school in the dark and cold wet weather and riding his bike on the dark roads. I told him he could do some work for me on a weekly basis and I would give him the equivalent of his paper round wage.

It worked well to begin with but Gary was not good with money and it went through his fingers like water. He would spend the whole week's wage in one go on something ridiculous. He simply had no value for money. I tried various things but all to no avail, and I felt the money he was getting came too easily. I eventually told him, 'Go and get your paper round, work hard for your money and you might value it a little more'.

He got his job and turned out early six mornings a week. He came back tired and often cold and wet, but he stuck at it and I had a new respect for him. It made no difference to his value for money though, for, despite working hard for it, he still spent it the instant he was paid, and mostly on ridiculous things. A trait that continued for the rest of his life.

As Gary got older he wanted designer clothes to impress his friends. The trouble was the prices of them were outrageous. I did him a deal: I would give him a clothes allowance per month and when it was gone it was gone.

Instead of spending one hundred pounds on a pair of trainers, if he bought a pair for fifty pound he still had fifty left to spend on something else. It was simple but effective and it worked brilliantly.

As Gary reached his final year at senior school he changed a little. Whilst he did well with his GCSEs things were beginning to slide a little, and he was becoming just a little bit rebellious. I just put it down to him being a teenager but, unbeknown to me at the time, he had begun to experiment with cannabis and, for the first time, the evil of drugs entered our lives.

Birthday at American Adventure

Best man for Dad

CHAPTER 3

It was around or just after this time when my wife and I were summoned to Gary's school to see the head teacher. We knew he was not doing well and it came as no surprise to be told his work had gone downhill to the point he wasn't even completing his work anymore. What did come as a surprise was to be told that he was becoming a disruptive influence in class, and it would be better for everyone concerned if he left the school. Perhaps we should have disagreed, but Gary was of leaving age and if he had no desire for further education perhaps it was the right thing to do. This was possibly my first mistake in a series of them, but I agreed and Gary left and began to look for work.

He had no idea of what he wanted to do or which direction to go in. There followed a period of unemployment, interspersed with several jobs, but he never really settled at any of them. This disconcerting period lasted a few years, drifting aimlessly in life, but he seemed happy enough in himself and, whilst I was obviously concerned, I felt sooner or later he would find his niche in life. It was at the end of this period that the bombshell finally dropped. Gary was taking drugs.

Neither my wife nor I had any experience with drugs and we had been totally unaware of what had been happening; we just assumed the problems had been down to teenage hormones. We still didn't realise the seriousness of it all. I thought it was just a phase and it would pass. How wrong could I have been?

Nevertheless we made Gary an immediate appointment at the drugs clinic and I went with him. Gary was teamed with his councillor and given a series of appointments. He admitted to taking cannabis and heroin, and his councillor, a gentleman called Nick, explained the seriousness of what he was doing, and we developed a plan of action to help Gary.

Things bumped along for several years. A lot of the time things were looking good and Gary was doing well, but at other times he returned to taking his drugs. I was still confident we could turn things around. I didn't know at this stage how evil and destructive these drugs really were. How could I have been so naïve?

When Gary was in his early twenties his behaviour deteriorated and things went rapidly downhill. He started taking money from family members and he refused to pay board. We didn't need the money, it was only a token, but Gary had to learn you couldn't freeload your way through life.

He began to smoke. I wasn't happy with it but he was an adult so we just asked him not to smoke in the house, but he continued to do so. He did as he pleased, and you couldn't reason with him. Something needed to be done.

My wife and I decided we couldn't carry on living like this, so we found Gary a flat that was a ten minute walk away. We paid the bond and the first month's rent and decorated it right through. We told Gary he could visit us any time he felt like it; he could come and have a meal with us and we would still do all his washing for him.

Gary was not particularly happy with the situation but he moved into the flat and things seemed to settle down for a while. It didn't rest easy with me that Gary was no longer living with us. I felt I had betrayed him. Some people told me that was ridiculous, and I had done more than most, that some people would have just thrown him out, but I knew I could have never have done that. I always knew I would try and do the right thing for my son.

His life consisted of highs and lows and in one of his low periods his landlord gave him notice, for the other tenants of the neighbouring flats complained of the noise and disturbance he and his so called friends were causing. The flat was a mess and we had to clean it up and redecorate, and we even had to rehang a door that had been ripped off its hinges. We found him another flat, but the same thing happened again and Gary found himself homeless.

We contacted various charities for the homeless and he began a phase in his life where he spent a night here and a night there. We still gave him food and did his washing. It was hard not to give him back his room at home but, as difficult as it was, we knew that it was not the long term answer to his problems.

I remember on one occasion, late one night, there was a knock at the door and when I opened it Gary just stood there looking at me. He asked if he could spend the night, as he had nowhere to go. He looked dreadful and he was cold and wet. The thing I wanted to do most in all the world was to put my arms around him, give him a hug, give him a bath and some food and a warm bed. How I refused him I still don't know, but I knew if he thought I would sort everything when things got really bad he would never break his cycle of self-destruction.

I turned him away and closed the door. I was devastated, heartbroken, and I sat and cried. What had I just done to my only son? How could I? If anything bad had happened to him that night I know I could never have lived with myself. Thankfully, it didn't, but it still disturbs me. All this upset was causing problems in the family; my mum and aunt couldn't understand what I was trying to achieve. They both fell out with me and we didn't speak or see each other for some time.

It would have been the easiest thing in the world for me to weaken and give Gary his room back. God knows I wanted to so badly, but I knew deep down it would do Gary no favours in the long term. I felt he had to hit rock bottom before he could begin to gain his own self-respect and put his life in order. After all, I wouldn't be there forever to pick up the pieces.

I wouldn't wish the agonies I went through on anyone. I just hoped and prayed I was doing the right thing.

I was still self-employed at that time and I had a busy work schedule to cope with. How I managed to get through all of it, I still don't know. I still saw Gary on a very regular basis. We still spent a lot of time together and I told him we would always be there for him, any problems to come and talk to me, and I would always try to do my best for him, but that he also had to help himself.

Fishing

Christmas at Grandma's

CHAPTER 4

After a short period of time Gary went to stay with my mum and aunt. I was secretly relieved he had somewhere safe to stay. I was so worried about him but I also knew it wasn't going to be a long term answer to his problems.

We all continued to help him with his drug problems and he was still attending the drug clinic. At times he was doing well and he was enjoyable to be with, and for spells we had the old Gary back with us. Unfortunately he still had periods where he went back to using drugs, and the old ways returned.

My mum and aunt couldn't cope with him living there anymore; they now realised what our life had been like. I couldn't face the worries of Gary being homeless again and once more we found him a flat.

Things went well for a period of time. He always had his underlying drug problem and we went through some bad periods, but we were coping. I helped him as much as I could. I had bailed him out several times with money when he got into debt. Some of the people he ended up owing money to were not nice people. My aunt also bailed him out on several occasions herself, one time for sixteen hundred pounds.

Should we have helped him or should we have just left him to suffer the consequences of his actions? Would it have ended badly or would it have taught him a valuable lesson? It's these questions that I have tortured myself with ever since. Personally, I don't think it would have altered his actions, and how can you watch your son, someone you love, being threatened and even beaten up?

I don't mind admitting it, I was out of my depth. I didn't know what to do for the best. I had taken charge of his money and paid all of his bills, I shopped with him to make sure he had food and he relied on me for pretty much everything financially. If he didn't have any money I reasoned he wouldn't be able to buy drugs. Unfortunately it didn't work. When he was not making my life a misery, badgering me for money, he was begging his grandmother and aunt. If all this failed he would borrow money from loan sharks and the first thing I knew about it was when he was being threatened, and had to pay back large sums of money.

I didn't know what to do next. We had got him back on the straight and narrow so many times, paid his debts and given him a new start, and every time he got himself in a mess yet again. All we could do was carry on helping him. Giving up on him was never an option.

I remembered when he was a tiny baby in the hospital and he fought so hard to stay alive. I couldn't fail him; I had to keep fighting just like he had done all those years ago.

It was at about this time that we heard his biological mother was to remarry. I wished her all the best because life had not been particularly kind to her in the past and she deserved some happiness. It was also around this time I lost my mum. She died suddenly of cancer. No one knew she had it until she was diagnosed two days before she died. My mum had gone into a coma so suddenly and without warning. It was a huge shock.

I know it's an obvious thing to say, but it is true, nevertheless, she had been there for me all my life. I had never known a time when my mum wasn't there and now suddenly she was gone. It was a strange feeling not having my mum around anymore. There had been no time for goodbyes, no time to prepare myself. I knew thousands of other people found themselves in the same position. I wasn't unique, but that thought didn't lessen the pain.

I think the loss of his grandmother hit Gary much harder than he liked to admit. She had played a huge part in his life ever since he had been born and I think it was fair to say the first person he had been really close to that he had lost.

Life continued in much the same way as before although we didn't have my mum around anymore. We experienced highs and lows with Gary, much as before. Unfortunately in one of the lows Gary lost his flat yet again, much for the same reasons as before. My aunt took him in again and he moved into my mum's old room, but he was made aware that it was only temporary.

Gary was also experiencing a few problems with the police. He got involved with a stolen car, although Gary was not involved with the actual theft. He was caught shoplifting, hoping to sell the goods to enable him to buy his drugs and various other offences. I repeatedly spoke up for him in court and requested for him to be given some help to try and sort his life out, and he was given a probationary sentence as well as fines.

It was at this period of his life that he took back a little control. He applied for a council flat away from his local area, the idea being to distance himself from some of his associates.

After a while, and with the help of his drug councillor and probation officer, he was eventually allocated a flat a little distance away. He started work with me as a plumber and heating engineer. I supplied him with a van and there was no shortage of work. I was impressed with how he worked. He was good at his job and he worked hard, his work was neat and he could solve problems intelligently. On the downside I could see why he'd had problems holding down his previous jobs. Gary had to be driven, he lacked motivation and, if he was left to his own devices, he would drift; he needed a guiding force.

Things continued quite well. He managed to keep off his drugs for long periods and every time he had a negative drugs test he was so proud of himself.

Unfortunately if Gary had some sort of perceived crisis in his life he couldn't cope well and he would eventually turn to his drugs to help him cope. He had been given all the support and all of the substitute drugs to help him. He even went on residential therapy courses, but he still turned to drugs in his times of crisis.

Life seemed to find a balance. He continued living in his flat and he also continued to work for me. He attended college on day release and did well. As I said before, he was quite intelligent even though some of the things he did made you think otherwise at times. He was also keeping his nose clean and had no more trouble with the police.

We turned our attentions from carp to catfish and it really caught our imagination. We fished all over England, as well as in France and Spain, and we both caught some monsters. Lots of people don't realise but there is much more to fishing than just catching fish: the closeness to nature, the friends you make along the way and, for Gary and myself, it was the quality time we spent together. We could enjoy ourselves away from the pressures and hassle of everyday life and, most importantly, away from the pressures of drugs.

We were obviously spending a great deal of time together through our work but we were spending equally the same time together in our leisure. If we weren't fishing we would be preparing our fishing tackle, wandering around tackle shops and even going to tackle shows. Sometimes we would be doing nothing special, just messing about.

We became really close. Our common interest bonded us together and although we were father and son we were more like best mates. There was nothing we would not do for one another.

On one occasion when leaving my aunt's house late one Friday night, a group of twelve or so young men were hanging around outside the house. My aunt had previous history with some of them and they began taunting her. Gary was with us and I told them both, 'Go inside and lock the door. Don't lower yourselves to their level by rising to them.' As I drove past them, one of them spat on my windscreen. It was disgusting and I was incensed. I slammed on my brakes and leapt out of the van – perhaps a foolish thing to do, but I was furious. I heard one of them say, 'Come on! We can take him; there's only him'. I wasn't worried, I was too angry and I told him, 'Come on then, try it, and I'll kick you so hard between your legs you'll be chewing your balls for a week,' Next second Gary was at my side. He had seen or heard the commotion and was there to help me in an instant. One of the young men wiped the spittle of my windscreen with his coat and it was over. Gary went inside and I drove off. Gary had no thought of danger for himself. He had seen that I might be in trouble and he was there for me. It was typical of the person he was.

It wasn't all sunshine and roses, of course. We had some real strong disagreements. They were purely verbal and when they were finished that was it, and it was forgotten about, and no grudges were ever held.

Gary still turned to his drugs in his times of need. We could never get him completely free of them, and they were a blight on our lives.

Gary and I came to an agreement which, while not ideal, seemed to be a compromise. I obviously didn't want him taking drugs in any way, shape or form, but if he couldn't leave them alone, I didn't want to be part of that world. I didn't want anything to do with Gary's drug taking. It had worn me down over the years and I refused to be involved. I told him if he got himself in debt for drugs, 'Don't come to me, the financial safety net is no longer there.' You have to remember that when Gary died he had been involved with drugs for twenty five years and I refused to be dragged down any further than I already had been.

If he spent his money on drugs sometimes he would have nothing left for food. It was no use me lending him or giving him the money to buy food, I might as well have bought him the drugs. It wasn't always easy to be strong, watching him go hungry, but I did it for the right reasons, and hoped he would eventually realise how stupid it all was. But unfortunately he never did. I told him I wouldn't help him financially any more. I probably should have done it sooner, but for everything else I would always be there for him. Life continued in much the same way for I guess around ten years. We had highs and lows but we got through it all.

Everything changed when I retired. Gary was given the van to use as his own and I told him, 'You do the jobs, and any problems with them, or you need an extra hand, I will always help.' Unfortunately, without me to motivate him on a daily basis, everything eventually went pear-shaped and he became unemployed once more.

It wasn't a problem in our relationship; we still continued to spend a lot of time with each other and we still went fishing. It may seem from what I have said that by spending my time with Gary I had been neglecting my wife. I had tried not to, and Elizabeth was very understanding, and we have a strong marriage. Nevertheless I was aware that it was bound to be putting a strain on it.

Elizabeth was having a difficult time with her mother, whom she was very close to, when she suffered a short illness, terminating in her sad demise. Elizabeth appeared to take it well but I know it hit her very hard.

Traditionally you are not supposed to get on well with your mother-in-law but in my case I did. She was a wonderful lady and she was sadly missed.

It was also around this time that my aunt, remember she had always been a second mum to me and also a second mum to Gary, started to have health problems which rapidly deteriorated. Gary was very close to his great aunt. She had been a big influence in his life.

He hadn't seen his biological mum for around ten years. I don't really know what happened, but his mum and her husband were living in rented accommodation. They seemed to move into different properties on a regular basis and I was also led to believe that their marriage was experiencing a few problems. Whatever the cause, on one of their many moves, she failed to let Gary have a phone number or an address, and he had no idea how to get in contact with her. He never saw her again. I don't want this to sound cruel, but she had never really been there for him, and you have to remember she was ill herself.

I would never have turned my back on Gary, anyway. If you love someone it's unconditional, but the situation with Gary's mum doubled my resolve to always stand by him and never leave him alone.

CHAPTER 5

My aunt's first real problems started when she damaged her Achilles tendon when out shopping. She could hardly walk and was pretty much house bound for almost six months. Kathleen, or Kath, as everyone called her, was still driving at this time but due to her injury she was unable to operate the pedals, so her car was garaged for the same amount of time.

Gary and myself visited regularly and obviously helped her as much as we could. We did her weekly shop and paid her bills at the bank and in fact did anything she needed.

When she became mobile again she seemed to have lost a lot of her confidence. I went out in her car with her but she seemed confused and, by her own admission, wasn't safe to drive. Kath decided to sell her car and after that she never drove again. Gary and I still did her weekly shop and she would just call at the supermarket for any small items she required.

We noticed Kath was beginning to forget things, small unimportant things at first, but she rapidly got worse. She hadn't noticed and insisted that there was nothing wrong, but I contacted her doctor and persuaded her to pay him a visit. Her doctor made her an appointment for a simple test and also a brain scan.

After her tests were completed she was given an appointment to receive her results. Both Gary and I attended the appointment with her. Kath was diagnosed with dementia and was told there was no cure, but with medication she would still be able to cope and live fairly normally for several years, if not longer.

Kath continued to deteriorate and Gary, without saying anything to anyone, gave up his flat and moved in to the spare room. I was aware that whilst Gary genuinely wanted to help, it was not a totally selfless act. He could live there fairly cheaply without his flat's rent, rates and fuel bills.

Gary also found himself a job at a local bakery, although he actually worked for an agency. He worked really hard, doing unsociable hours and loads of extra shifts. He was also working hard helping to look after my aunt and as her health deteriorated, he tackled jobs that I wouldn't have wanted to do.

Eventually we had to contact social services to obtain some care and supervision as Kath was becoming unfit to be left alone for long periods of time. For a while she refused to leave the house, even for a short while when the weather was nice. Social services tried to involve her in various activities but Kath would have none of it and basically became housebound.

Throughout this period Gary continued to work hard at his job at the bakery and hoped eventually to work for them instead of the agency. He was doing well and I hoped he had turned a corner in his life, but I was also aware he was still taking his drugs when he felt depressed.

Events continued in much the same way for well over a year until one morning I was contacted by her care worker to say that Kath had fallen in the night, and could I go over. I arrived quickly and it was obvious Kath, who was lying on the bedroom floor, needed extra help. I dialled 999 and the paramedics arrived and took her to the hospital. Gary had been working on one of his night shifts so he had not been there to help.

Kath had not injured herself in the fall apart a few bruises, but she was kept in hospital for over two months. Her health deteriorated to the point where she couldn't return to her home and I had to find her a care home. I settled on a care home that I thought was suitable and she was transferred there from hospital. Although I felt she was looked after really well, her health continued to deteriorate and after a few months she couldn't even get out of her bed.

Gary and I visited regularly but Kath didn't know where she was, and kept asking for Jessie —her sister, my mum. It was pointless telling her she died fifteen years ago, as it would only upset her, and she would ask the same question ten minutes later. We told her she was probably downstairs and Kath would say, 'Yes, perhaps she's gone to work.'

Kath told the staff at the care home that she still lived at the family home with her mum and dad, both of which had actually died in the fifties and sixties. When I visited her I would say, 'What have you been up to today then, Kath?' and she would always reply, 'Not a lot, just had a walk up town'. I would ask her, just to make conversation, 'Have you bought much?' 'Not a lot,' she would say. She was obviously away with the fairies but she kept her dignity for the most part and was well looked after, so I didn't feel she was suffering, but she certainly hadn't got a life worth living.

Kath got to the point where she was eating virtually nothing and she became a living skeleton. She had worked hard for over fifty years, and had stayed on at her job as a leather machinist for many years after she could have retired. Her money was running out and soon the care home fees would have needed paying from her half share of the family home in which Gary still lived. My mum had left her half to me when she died, and Kath and I had jointly owned the house for fifteen years.

I was called into the care home office on one of my many visits and told my aunt's death was imminent and so we made the relevant preparations. We all knew it was coming and it was going to be a relief. My aunt hadn't been alive for several years, she was just existing.

A few days later at midnight on 1st August 2015 I received a phone call to say Kath was near the end, and I should go over to be with her. I arrived within fifteen minutes of the call and Kath was lying peacefully in bed, breathing gently and to all intents and purposes asleep. I spoke to her but she showed no response and if she knew I was there I have no idea.

Someone brought me a cup of tea and I sat by her bed watching her breathing. The television was on, as the carers said the noise would have been a comfort to her. I had only been with her for ten minutes when I glanced at something on the television. I only glanced briefly but when I looked back at Kath she had stopped breathing. There was no noise, no movement. She had gone so peacefully.

Kath had been a second mum to me for sixty-five years and had been such a big part of my life. I had been willing her to die for months. I hadn't felt she was suffering, but she wasn't living either and it was a blessing. I thought I was prepared. I had known this moment was coming for such a long time but I wasn't, and I sat by her bed and silently cried.

I had tried to contact Gary as soon as I had received the call but I had been unable to contact him. He worked odd hours and couldn't always answer the phone. I rang him early the next morning and told him the sad news. He, like me, had known it was coming and he seemed very matter of fact. He told me he had sat with her when we were told her death was imminent and he had said his goodbyes then, but I knew her death would hit him hard. I don't think I realised how hard.

We organised the funeral between us and everything went as well as it could have. I had taken a power of attorney out for Kath several years before and all her funeral affairs were settled with no problems. She had left everything she owned to me, including her half of the family home, and I was now the sole owner of the property.

I include the forthcoming poem our 'Twilight Years' in my book because it was inspired by the death of my Aunt Kath and the loss of so many other much loved family members, also because, the death of my son Gary seemed to bring home to me, not only, my own mortality but also the fact that time was now passing so quickly, and I realised that I was in the Autumn of my years

OUR TWILIGHT YEARS

Our hopes all once so new
They seem to lie forlorn.
As our lifetimes actions we review
It is our twilight not our dawn.

The plans we made the future clear.
Life changed, we lost our zest,
Times that simply held no fear.
Did we really give them of our best?

Time then it was our special friend.
It's passing seemed so slow
It lay before us with no end
But now where does it go.

The years run down before our eyes
They pass so quickly now it seems
We have to say so many goodbyes
A sad reminder of our lost dreams.

Our coming years they seem so few
We need to make them last.
What can we do to see them through?
To stop them speeding past.

David Michael Straw

CHAPTER 6

I thought by contrast to the rest of this book I might introduce a chapter that is, shall we say, somewhat lighter. What follows is a few examples of the laughs Gary and I had along life's path. Some of the humour is lost in the actual telling of the story and, as the saying goes, 'You had to be there' to fully appreciate it. Nonetheless I think they are worth recounting. None of them are hilariously funny in the telling but are just a few of the many incidents I remember from the countless ones that actually took place.

My Aunt Kath was going on holiday and Gary, as a very small child, was at the house to see her departure. Kath had made quite a big thing of telling Gary how she was going to the airport to get on an aeroplane and fly to another country.

As Kath got in the taxi Gary was in my mum's arms to wave her farewell. The taxi pulled away and as my mum and Gary watched it drive away, just by chance, a plane appeared in the sky. Gary pointed to it and with a little grimace and a groan he lamented, 'Oh, no. Kath's missed it.'

One mealtime, when Gary was around five years old, we were at the dinner table, just the two of us, having a meal. I had prepared a cauliflower cheese and also given Gary a glass of water with his meal. I felt he should drink more water than he did and I encouraged him to do so. As the meal progressed the water remained untouched. 'Have a drink of your water,' I told him, but it was to no avail; his glass still remained full. Trying again, I said, 'Go on, Gary, have a drink of your water,' and, thinking on my feet, I added, 'It's good for your liver.' He looked at me, then down at his meal and then back to me once more. His eyes wide open and full of innocence he replied, 'I haven't got any liver; it's cauliflower cheese.'

On another occasion when he was a little older, he and his group of friends decided it would be a good idea to go boating on a certain lake that we knew. Gary had a fairly large inflatable two-man dinghy and one of his friends had a smaller one. We inflated them in the garden and with the aid of a puncture repair kit managed eventually to make them airtight. We placed the smaller dinghy on the van roof, Gary's on top of that, and then I lashed them down. Off we went, six or seven kids in the back, Gary in the front and the dinghies on top.

On route to the lake we had to travel down a busy dual carriageway and, as we drove along at about sixty to seventy miles an hour, I heard a shout and then howls of laughter from the back. I quickly looked in my rear view mirror and saw to my horror a dinghy ascending high in the air and then slowly floating back to earth with an exaggerated side-to-side movement, with cars swerving either side of it, before landing right in the middle of the road.

By the time I managed to stop safely I was a few hundred yards further along the road. I leapt out, sprinted as fast as I could back to the dinghy, watching all the high-speed cars swerving around it, thinking, *If the police appear now I've had it.*

I arrived at the scene and, sprinting between the cars, I retrieved the dinghy as quickly as I could. As I raced back up the road, almost buried beneath the dinghy, I thought if the police see me now they will still want to know what I am doing running along a dual carriageway with a fully inflated dinghy on my back. I eventually reached the van and retied the dinghy back on top, hopefully making a better job of it this time. I jumped back in my van, waited for a break in the traffic and then drove off. I had got away with it. The kids in the back and Gary, of course, were in fits of laughter, and the incident was well talked about for a long time afterwards.

Also around that time Gary and I did the weekly shop before dropping in to see my mum and aunt. On returning home, Gary was helping me to put away the shopping in the kitchen cupboards. At this point may I explain that our kitchen floor is Ruabon-tiled and they are like bell metal, drop a cup and it's in a thousand pieces. As Gary passed me the various items to store in the cupboard, he picked up a very large jar of pickled onions. 'Oh no,' I hear you say but unfortunately, 'Oh yes.' As Gary lifted up the jar above his head to pass it to me, it slipped through his fingers and hit the floor like an exploding bomb.

We were both covered in pickled onions and vinegar. He looked at me, his eyes full of fear and trepidation, but what could I say? It was an accident. We cleaned up the mess. It took forever and we were finding pickled onions for days, and the house smelled like malt vinegar for weeks!

Gary was around eight years old when we both went on a rather eventful camping holiday in Cornwall. We broke down on the M5 and it cost a fortune to have the van repaired and then, in the middle of the night, whilst at Tintagel, the tent, which was a big frame tent, was utterly destroyed in a gale. The rain was bucketing down and the wind was howling in from the sea when the tent gave up the ghost and collapsed, the frame bent and buckled.

We threw everything in the back of the van in the pitch blackness, all the while getting soaked in the process. We then had to sit in the front of the van and wait for daylight; it seemed to take an awfully long time to arrive. The rest of the holiday had to be spent in a boarding house with a very strange landlady.

The next incident I want to tell you about happened on a day out. I can't remember where it was now but that is of little matter. As we wandered along the seafront, looking in the shops, I was carrying an unopened two litre bottle of Lilt. It was a red hot day and I had bought the bottle to quench our thirst but as of yet we hadn't had a drink. As we passed one of the shops, I think it was Gary who decided to stop and look in the window. To set the scene I will first describe the shop. It consisted of two large plate glass windows with the door in between. The door was not level with the windows but set back about ten feet. It made an entrance of about ten foot long by six foot wide before you actually entered the shop door. The sides were again plate glass windows and the floor completely tiled. We were both standing well inside this area when the bottle of Lilt slipped through my fingers and fell to the floor. It landed upright, bounced once more and then landed on its side. It was a plastic bottle and, instead of shattering, it blew the screw top clean off the bottle. Its contents sprayed out under pressure, sending the bottle round and round in circles like a demented Catherine wheel, not stopping until it was empty. We both watched in fascination until it stopped spinning. The ceiling, the windows, the door, the floor and ourselves were covered in two litres of Lilt. Instead of doing the sensible and responsible thing, like going into the shop and apologising, we both looked at each and then, if you excuse the pun, we bottled it and ran as fast as our legs would carry us, going back to the van by a different route so we didn't have to pass the shop again.

On one occasion when Gary and I were fishing at one of our favourite lakes, just as it was dropping dark, Gary had a run on one of his rods. At the time we were both sitting in front of my bivvy, just enjoying the evening and having a beer. Gary used to smoke at that time and he always bought rolling tobacco and rolled his own cigarettes. When his alarm sounded we both jumped up and went across to his rods. Gary's pouch of tobacco must have been on his knee and, as he got up, it must have fell in the water, but in all the excitement we didn't notice. Gary landed the fish, a forty plus catfish, and after we had weighed, photographed and returned it, he put his bait out into the lake once again. This must have taken a good thirty minutes, after which we returned to our chairs. That was when he noticed the full pouch of tobacco in the water. After all this time you can imagine it was soaked through, but Gary had no other tobacco, so he was in a dilemma. After much muttering and cursing, he went over to his bivvy, while I remained sitting in my chair. Gary's bivvy was a little way up the bank and I didn't pay attention to what he was doing. After about ten minutes or so I noticed a really strange smell drifting along the bank. At first it smelled like bacon frying, followed by something that smelled like someone was setting fire to a load of old socks. I got up and wandered across to see what was happening. Gary had his frying pan on the stove and was trying to dry out his tobacco. Unfortunately, it kept burning and, combined with the aroma of the bacon that had been cooked previously in the pan, it smelled awful.

When he had dried it out the best he could, which took a while, he rolled a cigarette and lit it. It smelt exactly as before, bacon and old socks. He pulled a face and declared it tasted disgusting, but he must have been desperate because he smoked the rest of the pouch. I made sure I was nowhere near him when he did so.

Before Gary came to work for me full time, on certain jobs he would come with me so he could have a little bit of money in his pocket. On one particular job we had fitted central heating and when we had finished, as we packed away, I told him to go around the job and check for leaks or any problems. He returned after a short time and reported that everything was fine and there were no leaks or other problems. As the job was a little distance from home I thought perhaps, just to be sure, I should check things for myself. As I looked around I saw that one of the radiator valves was leaking and water was dripping onto the floor, forming a puddle. I called Gary over to show him the leak and, as I reprimanded him on his carelessness, told him that it would probably have meant an out-of-hours callout to fix the problem. He looked me straight in the eye and, with an absolutely straight face, and in all sincerity, told me, 'Well, you get what you pay for.' Considering I was only paying him peanuts, I couldn't really argue with that.

Only a few winters ago Gary and I went pike fishing at a local lake and as we both sat waiting for a take, Gary said, 'Wow that's a big lad.' I looked up to see someone walking across the field, complete with all of his fishing gear. He was indeed a big lad; in fact extremely overweight. He ended up fishing fairly close to us and we spent several hours in conversation with him; he seemed a really nice guy. Judging by the amount of food he had brought with him for his lunch it was certainly no mystery to why he was so large. At the end of the day we said our goodbyes to our new friend and went our separate ways.

Just a few weeks later the club who owned the lake were having their A.G.M and, because they wanted to turn the lake into a syndicate water, Gary and I both attended. The first person we saw as we entered the building was our new overweight friend. We both said hello and after a brief conversation the meeting began. Among other topics the bailiff of the lake wanted to introduce a ban on fishing as soon as the carp in the lake started to spawn, but because the spawning time was so variable it would be left to the bailiff's discretion. The committee would have none of it and every argument the bailiff put forward the committee dismissed. After a while the bailiff conceded defeat but, in a final show of frustration, he retorted, 'Well, it's up to you but all I can say is how would you like it when you were having sex if someone started throwing food at you?' As quick as a flash and without a pause our new friend, the overweight guy, punched his hand in the air and exclaimed in a loud voice, 'Well, I wouldn't mind.' Because of his size and his obvious love for food it was just so funny; the whole room was in hysterics.

Gary and I didn't get our wishes because the lake was turned into a syndicate water, but it was worth the effort to attend just for the laugh.

I could go on and tell you so many more stories of the times Gary and I shared together but suffice to say, they were all special and memorable times.

Just one final short story. This one is not humorous, in fact, I find it rather poignant and it will gently return you to the general mood of the following chapters of this book. If you travel along the A6 from Ambergate to Matlock you will eventually arrive at what I call Cromford crossroads, but before you do, as you travel along the A6 you will pass along a stretch of road on a long curving bend. The trees grow thickly along either side of this stretch of road and the branches meet overhead. When fully in leaf they allow little light to pass through. When travelling along this stretch of road many years ago, when Gary was a young child, he seemed quite transfixed and he commented, 'It's like being in a tunnel.' Ever since that time it was always known to us as Gary's tunnel.

Now almost forty years later the same scenario still applies and whenever I travel through it those words still echo in my mind: 'It's like being in a tunnel' and I always think quietly to myself, *We're in Gary's tunnel.*

I thought we were just having fun.

I didn't know we were making memories.

Gary and I didn't get our wishes because the lake was turned into a syndicate water, but it was worth the effort to attend just for the laugh.

I could go on and tell you so many more stories of the times Gary and I shared together but suffice to say, they were all special and memorable times.

Just one final short story. This one is not humorous, in fact, I find it rather poignant and it will gently return you to the general mood of the following chapters of this book. If you travel along the A6 from Ambergate to Matlock you will eventually arrive at what I call Cromford crossroads, but before you do, as you travel along the A6 you will pass along a stretch of road on a long curving bend. The trees grow thickly along either side of this stretch of road and the branches meet overhead. When fully in leaf they allow little light to pass through. When travelling along this stretch of road many years ago, when Gary was a young child, he seemed quite transfixed and he commented, 'It's like being in a tunnel.' Ever since that time it was always known to us as Gary's tunnel.

Now almost forty years later the same scenario still applies and whenever I travel through it those words still echo in my mind: 'It's like being in a tunnel' and I always think quietly to myself, *We're in Gary's tunnel.*

I thought we were just having fun.

I didn't know we were making memories.

CHAPTER 7

Gary was still living at the house and after Kath's death I felt it was important to get his affairs sorted. I told Gary what I had planned and he was quite agreeable. I approached a letting agency and everything was set in motion, a contract was drawn and a reasonable monthly rent agreed. I felt it was important to establish the renting on a formal and legal footing. Gary was earning decent money and because of his lack of ability to handle money, I knew it would be sensible.

I obviously didn't want to make money out of my own son but I felt he should have responsibility. I told him once we have a small sum of money set aside for repairs or such things as a replacement boiler, we would invest all the rent money in renovating the property and bring everything up to a high standard. I also told him that when anything happened to me, the house would be his, so he was investing in his own future.

Elizabeth and I had in the past discussed what would happen to Gary when we were no longer here. We both felt leaving him to his own devices with a large sum of money was not the best idea. With him having the house, we felt that if the money was placed in a trust for him there would be money available for all his essentials. Gary would have a roof over his head, his rates and fuel bills paid and food on the table. We knew it wasn't foolproof but, because there would be no one else about to look after him, it was going to be our best option.

At first things went well but, after a short time, the rent wasn't being paid on time; it always came but very often in dribs and drabs. Although he was earning decent money, he was obviously spending much of it on other things.

Gary had quite a large circle of friends, most of them decent people, but I also knew most of them were drug users. I had done everything possible in the past to get him away from drugs, and I knew being with other drug addicts was far from ideal. He was approaching forty years of age and I couldn't dictate who he made friends with.

Gary was still working for the agency but full time at the same bakery. He had been there a good while and I think he was well thought of as a worker. He was hoping to be taken on to actually work for the bakery directly. The bakery had a no drug policy and Gary took several tests, as did everyone else there, and they were negative.

One of Gary's friends, who was taking drugs himself, inherited quite a large amount of money, and I knew he wasn't spending it wisely. For Gary and his friends it became party time. Obviously I was concerned, but Gary seemed to be doing reasonably well and, after twenty five years of trying to wean him off drugs, I had become very tired. I tried to interfere, but what could I do? Gary was a man and, because he still saw his drugs worker on a regular basis, I just hoped things would settle down.

On one of the bakery's drug tests Gary was found to be positive and so he lost his job. He was quite upset, as he really enjoyed his job and he had been on the verge of being employed directly. It seemed to settle him down for a while and he soon found another job, but they were really unsociable hours, and it was just a stop gap until he could find something better.

Both Gary and I wanted to begin renovating his home and I told him that the first thing we needed to do was to clear out the clutter going back to when my mum and aunt lived there. Gary had previously had a friend move into the spare room, the idea being that his friend would pay towards rent and fuel bills, and therefore ease Gary's financial burden. At first, although I didn't want to interfere, things worked well. His friend was unemployed and whilst Gary was at work, his friend would keep the house clean and do most of the cooking. After a while the situation broke down and his friend left to live with his mum again, and Gary was left on his own.

Although the house was a bit of a mess it wasn't too bad, and I told Gary to give it a spruce up and we would clear the clutter and then renovate it. Unfortunately, it never happened. Every time I pressed him he told me it was still a tip so not to come in at the moment until he had cleaned it up. I went along with this. It was all too easy for me, and it was Gary's home and if he wanted to live that way that was up to him. In hindsight, it was one of my biggest mistakes. I should have taken control.

We still spent a lot of time fishing, which we both loved, or simply doing nothing special. We were still the best of friends and were really close. In hindsight, I had let things slip, had taken my eye off of the ball. On the face of it everything seemed to be going reasonably well. Yes, I knew he was still doing drugs but he had been doing drugs for twenty-five years, and I accepted it. I had tried everything in my power to alter it, but I had always failed, and it was easier to turn a blind eye.

Looking back, I should have seen the signs; they were obvious enough if I had taken the time to look. I loved my son dearly. We had been through so much together but, as I said before, twenty-five years of Gary's drug taking had taken its toll on me. I was tired and I didn't want the hassle of it anymore.

On 1st September Gary was forty and I wanted to get him something special for his birthday, but I knew if I gave him cash he would probably spend it on drugs, and if I bought him anything it would probably be pawned for drug money, so I left it and gave him nothing. There was plenty of time to make things right in the future; at least that's what I thought.

Why hadn't I done something positive? But in my defence what could I have done that I had not tried to do before? Even if I had known the house was in such a state, even if I had helped him clean it all and start again, what would it have achieved? I had sorted his affairs out so many times before, got him back on an even keel. Would it have been any different this time? I doubted it would but, looking back, I can't forgive myself for not trying.

Christmas came and we all had a really nice family Christmas and, apart from Gary's so-called sciatica, he seemed really well. My birthday is on the 30th December and we had a nice family day together. Gary bought me a fishing video and we watched it together. I said to him, 'You know you aren't as daft as you look. You buy me a present and you get as much out of it as I do.' He looked at me and laughed and replied, 'That's right.' Ironically, the video was from a series of cat-fishing videos in France and Spain and Gary had bought me a couple of them on previous occasions.

As I opened this one he told me he didn't know which of the remaining series he should have got me but he said, 'It doesn't really matter because we'll get them all eventually.' I didn't know at that moment, of course. But we were never given the time.

Over the next seven to ten days due to Gary's work commitments and my own schedule we didn't see a lot of each other, but it didn't matter much at the time. After all, we had our fishing holidays booked and the rest of our lives to spend together. Little did I realise the horrors that were about to unfold, not only for myself but also for Gary.

CHAPTER 8

When I look back on the events of which I am to describe I find them so very cruel and extremely hard to come to terms with.

I met Gary on the afternoon of the 11th January. He was waiting for me outside his house and, as I pulled up in the car, he came over and opened the car door and the words that greeted me were, 'Can you lend me two hundred pounds until I get paid on the 24th?' I told him no way, but he persisted, begging me to lend him the money. It was supposedly for a drug dealer whom he owed. I still refused but suggested we go for a drink and a chat. We ended up at McDonalds and I bought us both a Coca Cola. We sat and chatted for a while then Gary's phone rang. He told me it was his drug dealer, and he was going to meet him and would be back shortly. True to his word, he returned after a few minutes and we continued chatting while we finished our drinks.

I ran Gary back up to his house. By then it was dark. He got out and stood illuminated by the car's interior light. He thanked me for the lift and started begging me to lend him the two hundred pounds. 'I'll never ask you again for money and I'll pay you interest on it,' he told me. Again I refused in no uncertain terms, and I will never forget that hopeless, pleading look on his face.

He said no more but gently closed the car door and walked away. He was wearing dark jeans and a black coat and the darkness swallowed him up. Although I didn't realise it at the time I would never see my son alive again. I drove away, obviously quite upset at the events but I knew lending him money wasn't an answer.

My mobile rang on Tuesday the twelfth, early evening. It was Gary and we had a chat and he asked me as usual, 'What have you had for your tea?' It eludes me now but I told him and then asked what had he eaten? 'Rice Snaps' was the answer. 'Never head of them,' I said and he told me they were cereals from Tesco. We continued talking for a while and then he began asking to borrow that money. I snapped back at him, 'Gary, I'm sick of hearing about money. I've told you NO,' and then I said, 'I'm going,' and switched off the phone.

I was never to speak to Gary again.

I left it for three days without ringing him; we had been there so many times before. Usually after three or four days he would text me an apology. *I'm sorry, I know I was out of order, it won't happen again. I am definitely going to sort myself out this time. I don't want to keep living like this,* and I believe he genuinely meant it.

On the Saturday 16th I rang him but only got voicemail, so I texted him, *Ring me please, let me know you are OK.'* No reply.

Same again on Sunday 17th and on the morning on Monday 18th. Still no reply. I was beginning to be concerned, but not unduly worried for, as I said we had been there so many times before.

After lunch I told my wife, Elizabeth, 'I'm going over to Ilkeston to see what Gary's up to.' I arrived at the house around 3pm, parked the car and knocked on the door. There was no answer and my thought was that if someone was chasing him for money he wouldn't answer anyway. I got out my key but I knew if he was in, his keys would be in the door as usual, and I wouldn't be able to gain entry. To my surprise I inserted the key, turned the lock and opened the door. I shouted his name but all was quiet and I presumed he was out, either at work or perhaps with his mates.

The house was squalid and my thought was *This isn't normal. Gary's in need of help.* Remember, I hadn't been in for a while, for he would always say, 'Don't come in, Dad, it's a tip. I'm going to clean it up before you see it.' My belief was he was out and I thought I would take the opportunity to have a look at the state of the place upstairs. He would be none the wiser.

I climbed the stairs. Gary's bedroom was on the left; the door was half open but the view into the room was obscured. As I opened the door fully the unmistakable sweet, sickly smell of death hit me. I hadn't smelt it since my grandfather's death in 1958, but I knew it instantly. At the same moment I saw Gary lying across the bed. I knew he was dead.

I rushed across the room and held him; he felt cold and stiff. A white foam had come from his mouth and run down his cheek and pooled on the bedsheet. His eyes wide open and staring as though in horror, he looked so small and deflated in death.

I knew it was too late to help him but he couldn't be dead, he just couldn't be. This was Gary, my son, my best friend.

I was hysterical. I screamed his name over and over and, between sobs I shouted, 'FOR F—K SAKE! NO, F—KING HELL! NO, YOU CAN'T BE DEAD!' I told myself to wake up, that this was a nightmare, but it wasn't, it was all too real. Never had I felt such despair, such hopelessness. I sat at the top of the stairs, crying uncontrollably, while I dialled 999. A woman's voice answered, asking which service I required. I could hardly speak but I replied, 'I don't know. I've just found my son dead.' 'Is he unconscious?' she asked. 'No,' I replied, 'he's dead.' She told me the ambulance was on its way and did I want her to stay on the line and talk to me? I didn't want to talk, I was numb. I could barely speak anyway. I was crying so much she hung up.

I rang my wife, Elizabeth, and just repeated over and over between my tears, 'He's dead, he's dead.' The rest of the conversation was a blur. I remember hearing my wife crying, and I switched off the phone.

I continued to sit there. I don't know for how long, time stood still. I was still crying uncontrollably when I heard a vehicle pull up outside the house, the blue light flashing and bouncing off the bedroom walls. I went downstairs and opened the front door before they even got out of the ambulance. Two young ladies entered, paramedics I presumed, and I led the way upstairs to my son. One of them began to examine Gary, the other led me downstairs and sat me down while we waited.

It was all surreal, it wasn't happening. The police arrived, statements were taken, arrangements made and I sat there, not believing what was happening. Surely I would wake up soon? The paramedics left and I was taken to Ilkeston police station to help make a detailed report. The police took me back to the house but I was not allowed inside. 'Sit in the car,' I was told, 'while you wait for the undertaker to come to remove the body.' How could he be described as a body? It was my son, Gary, someone I loved more than life itself, someone I had looked after and watched over for forty years. Surely it must be a mistake, it couldn't be anything else could it?

I've got to wake up soon, I just have to.

I didn't sit in the car. I walked up and down the street for over an hour. It was dark and it was freezing, but it didn't really register. I was still numb.

Eventually the undertaker arrived and they went into the house. After what seemed an age they came out. It didn't matter how long they took. I wasn't going anywhere until I knew Gary had been looked after.

Gary was carried out on a stretcher zipped up in a body bag and he was placed in the back of what was basically a van. The doors slammed shut and he was driven away. I watched in disbelief, my mind still not accepting what I knew to be true, unless of course I was still dreaming. Surely that could still be possible? I was clinging on to the fact that it might be a dream. *Oh, please tell me it's possible, because I can't bear it otherwise.*

The vehicle neared the end of the road, its orange indicator light flashing, its intention to turn left and then the glare of its red brake lights as it slowed. Everything was blurred by the tears in my eyes. It stopped briefly and then suddenly it was gone, just as suddenly as Gary had gone from my life. It had vanished and my son Gary had vanished with it. Its disappearance seemed to emphasise something that mere words could never describe, something that had gone forever and could never be replaced.

I stood there in the freezing cold and the darkness of the night, my mind in chaos, and my thoughts blurred until I slowly returned to what now seemed a very cruel and desolate world. I waited for what seemed like an age as the police finished whatever they were doing inside the house. I was still not allowed inside.

When they finally emerged, they asked if there was anyone waiting for me at home. I told them, 'Yes, my wife.' They locked the door, handed me the keys and told me to take care driving home.

I was on my own.

It was over. My son was dead and I had to somehow get through the rest of my life without him. I couldn't even think about the rest of my life.

How could I even get through the night, through the darkness? Not only the darkness of that night but also the darkness within me?

I got in my car and somehow drove home, tears pouring down my face. I knew I wasn't going to wake up, my nightmare was real.

When I arrived home after 9.30pm my wife and two friends who had sat with her were waiting for me. They all gave me a hug but nothing helped. How could it? After a short while our friends left and my wife and I sat crying, talking about Gary, but mainly crying. I was desolate.

Eventually Elizabeth went to bed but I knew I couldn't be there in the dark; my mind was in turmoil, so many thoughts. I decided to watch the television. I had to do something. I played some old reruns of Only Fools and Horses Christmas specials, and it amazed me to hear myself laugh occasionally. How could that be possible amidst so much grief, so much sorrow and I could still laugh? That couldn't be right. I turned the television off. By now it was 5am on the 19th; what could I do with myself?

I slipped on my coat and shoes and went outside. It was dark and white over with frost and I started to walk. I didn't know where I was going; it didn't matter but I had to go somewhere. I walked to Ilkeston, a walk that Gary had done so many times in his life. I walked through the darkness, tears pouring down my face. I passed all the places where I used to pick Gary up in the car. I visualised him standing there waiting for me. I visited Tesco where Gary had worked, I saw the bakery, the machine that cooked the chickens and I could still see him there doing his job.

I walked past Gary's house, the scene of so much anguish just a few hours ago, now in darkness and empty, nobody there, no Gary and there never would be again. I walked homeward along the canal the way Gary would have walked on his way to visit me, a walk he would have done so many times, a place we had fished together.

It was still dark, and anyone could have been waiting. I could have been robbed, beaten, even thrown in the canal, but I didn't care. What would it matter? If someone could have killed me I would have welcomed it, I was so consumed by grief.

As I neared home the sun rose with a glorious red sky. I suppose it was quite beautiful but I couldn't appreciate it; there was no room in my heart for beauty it was full of sadness and so much sorrow. I slipped the key in the door at home and opened up. Elizabeth was waiting for me, frantic with worry. She had searched the house and the garden, wondering if she herself would find a body, my body. I hadn't thought, I was too lost in my own grief.

As I had walked home people had been going to work, things were continuing as normal. How could that be? Gary was gone, my life changed forever and yet to everyone else it was just an ordinary day. Did no one realise the enormity of what had happened?

Overleaf is the opium poppy,

How could something so pure

So beautiful

Be turned into something that creates so much grief,

So much sorrow?

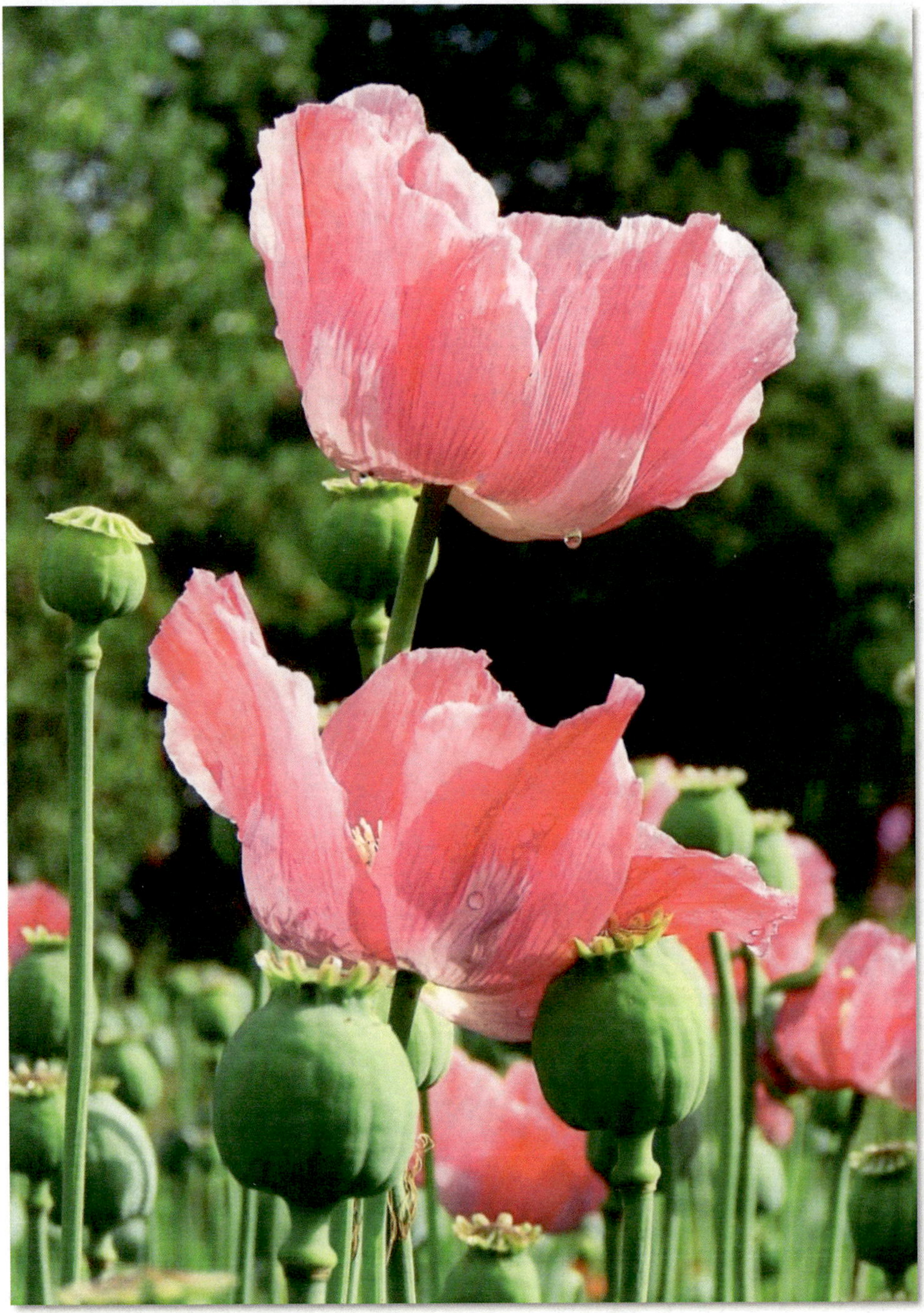

For all the times I was not there,

I am so sorry.

For all the times I did not listen,

I am so sorry.

For all the times I did not understand,

I am so sorry.

For all the times I did not show I loved you,

I am so sorry.

For all of time,

I am so sorry.

David Michael Straw

The following few lines are not a poem or a eulogy, in fact I don't really know what they are, so perhaps it's best to describe them simply as a thought.

I have entitled them

AN ORDINARY DAY

What is death? Such a relatively short word, an innocuous word, but one which has few rivals in its consequences? Is it the beginning or the end? Is it the start of a new and wonderful existence on a higher plain, reunited with all our loved ones from the past, or is it a black hole of oblivion? What we believe, of course, will depend upon our faith.

We don't always see death coming and death has no qualms over whom it chooses. It doesn't differentiate between the rich or the poor, it doesn't matter about your beliefs or your faith, it can choose anyone, but the day we die begins just as an ordinary day.

Millions of people will awake, have their breakfast, just an ordinary day. But for those whom death has chosen and their loved ones everything changes. There will be sorrow, there may be regret and recriminations, and there may even be relief, but the one sure thing is that, for those concerned, nothing will ever be the same again, and it all began with just an ordinary day.

CHAPTER 9

What do I do now? Everything seemed so unreal, as though it was happening to someone else; it still seemed unbelievable that Gary was gone. How could it have happened so suddenly? No warning, not even a thought it could have been possible.

My whole world turned upside down in the space of those few seconds when I found Gary, and there wasn't a single thing I could do to alter it.

I needed to let people know but I couldn't trust myself to speak, so I asked Elizabeth to start ringing people and tell them what was, to me, almost unbelievable. And, of course, I needed to contact Gary's biological mum, my first wife. She hadn't seen Gary for fifteen years at least and after she remarried she would not give her own son a telephone number or address to contact her. She had recently sent him cards and letters and ironically over the last couple of months Gary had been given her phone number. He had called her and had a few conversations. I needed to let her know, but I didn't feel it was right to do it over the phone. I didn't have her number anyway.

After making enquiries I discovered where she was living and Elizabeth and I visited her and gave her the sad news. Her own health had deteriorated so much since I had last seen her, and I was quite shocked at what I saw.

She was understandably upset and, as we left, I promised I would keep her informed of all relevant details of funerals, autopsies and anything else remotely connected to Gary. I needed to arrange the funeral, and rang the Cooperative funeral care, the people who just a short while before had organised Kath's funeral. Little did I think I would be organising my own son's funeral such a short time later.

I spoke to Caroline, a lady both Gary and myself had met when we had organised Kath's funeral. When I told her of Gary's death she seemed genuinely shocked and concerned about how I was feeling. We arranged an appointment for the following day and, because she had known Gary, it seemed a little more personal and, for some reason, that seemed to help just a little.

I remember very little of the days that followed. They were a blur of people speaking to me over the phone to offer their condolences, people visiting me to see how I was and sympathy cards dropping through the letter box. I suppose I was still in shock. It was all just happening, and I appeared to be watching from a distance as though somehow detached.

How I got through those early days I have no idea. I cannot begin to describe how I felt. Just think of your worst nightmare and multiply it a hundred-fold and it still doesn't come close.

The appointment at the funeral directors went well enough and all the arrangements were made. I didn't really want anything to do with the funeral; it was as if making the arrangements somehow meant I was accepting Gary's death.

The service was arranged for 17th February as far ahead as was practical. I couldn't face it; I didn't want to be a part of any of it; I didn't want to choose coffins, flowers, music or any other details. Gary was dead and all of this seemed so unreal, so inconsequential, and I didn't want to be taking part in organising any of the arrangements.

I always intended to go to the service but to sit at the back of the chapel and take no part in it. I would let everything pass me by so that it wasn't really happening. That same day I received a call from the coroner's office saying they had received Gary's body and they would carry out an autopsy the following morning and would give me a call in the afternoon.

I spent the whole of the following morning thinking of how my son was being sliced open, his organs being removed, examined and weighed, and all the other clinical things that had to be done. I realised it was necessary, but surely it would have been better not to know when it was happening?

The phone call came as promised at approximately 12.20pm and I was told the results would take two to three weeks. In reality it turned out to be almost eight weeks before I was to even begin to get any answers.

The days and nights passed slowly. I lived them or rather endured them a day at a time.

A friend of Gary and myself, who was a police officer, came with me to Gary's address to see if we could find anything that could begin to answer all the questions that were going through my mind. I knew the house was squalid when I had found Gary's body, but not until I went into the house this time did I realise how bad it really was. There were hypodermic needles everywhere, both new and used, blood-soaked clothes on the furniture and floor, blood spatters on the walls and kitchen appliances, filthy pots and pans piled in the sink and rubbish scattered everywhere. Every room in the house was in a disgusting state. How could I have let things get so bad? Why hadn't I gone into the house more often?

I was ashamed of myself. I didn't blame Gary, Gary was vulnerable. This was my fault and my fault alone and I would have to live with that knowledge and guilt for the rest of my life. I had let my son down and, yes, I realise it was his own lifestyle choice, but I could and should have done more. People told me it wasn't my fault but I knew in my heart that it was, and that it was something I could never come to terms with.

My friend confirmed this was not Gary's mess alone, but the house had been turned into a drug den for who knows how many people. What a mess, and I had let it happen. I was so naïve.

So many things were going through my mind. I missed my son, my best friend. How could it be possible I would never see him again, never speak to him again? I was overcome with grief and sorrow and, I suppose, self-pity. This should never have happened. Why had I taken things for granted? Why had I not been more vigilant? Why hadn't I rung Gary sooner? Why had I not lent him that two hundred pounds? Why had I not gone to the house? I needed answers to all these questions in my head. I had to try to find those answers.

Gary last attended work on Tuesday evening, the 12th January. That meant nothing in itself, he could have been feeling unwell, so not attended. The last time I spoke to him was that same evening, when he had rung on his mobile around 7pm and we had shared a few of our jokes about what we had eaten for our evening meals. Gary had eaten a bowl of cereals, Rice Snaps to be exact; Gary loved his cereals. The conversation had eventually turned to money and again he begged me to lend him that two hundred pounds. I told him again in no uncertain terms there would be no money and that I was sick of hearing him beg for money. Then tired of his pleading, I'd told him, 'Anyway, Gary, I'm going' and switched off the phone.

I was never to speak to my son again, never again to hear his voice. If only I could have known; switching the phone off on him so abruptly, something else I have to live with.

Gary had been to the pharmacy on the following day, the 13th January. There were no outgoing calls or texts on his phone after this date.

The box of rice snaps was still almost full and there was milk in the fridge. I had found Gary's body on the 18th January, so why had none since the 12th been eaten? When had Gary died? How long had he been lying dead and cold, all alone? Had he died quickly or had he lain for hours feeling unwell and dying, not able to get help? Was it an overdose, or was it some bad drugs? Had he done it on purpose because it all became too much to bear and he couldn't take anymore?

I had to find out all I could, I needed to know as many facts as possible. My mind would never be at rest and I needed to know.

I arranged a meeting with his key worker. I rang some of his friends who I knew had shared drugs with him. I rang the police to see if their investigation had led anywhere, but none of it shed any more light on the situation. I wasn't a lot wiser than at the beginning.

Suddenly the waters became a lot murkier. It appeared from some of his texts he had begun to deal a few drugs, supposedly for the drug dealer he owed money to. He had been given drugs to sell, but had used them himself and that was why he owed money.

As I checked his mail, mainly bills, I found a letter from Europe Car demanding the return of the hire car that had supposedly been hired on the 8th January. The letter did not look official, no-one knew of any car. Was this someone, the drug dealer perhaps, trying to make contact with someone close to Gary to get back the money Gary owed? I didn't want to ring the number on the letter from Europe Car. If it was the drug dealer then he would know how to contact me, so I passed all of the information on to the police.

Had Gary been pressured, had the drug dealer actually harmed or even killed Gary? Perhaps it was ridiculous but my mind was in overdrive, and perhaps I watched too much television. I couldn't do anything but wait for the autopsy report and hope that might shed a little light on all that had happened, but that was weeks away. How could I wait that long?

So many questions that I knew may never be answered. I was coping at the moment, but only just and for how much longer?

Death can seem so cruel,

We fear its coming,

Yet it is ever present in our lives.

But is it the pariah we believe?

For without death there can be no life,

Without life there can be no love,

And without love there is nothing.

David Michael Straw

CHAPTER 10

I was so upset, so grief stricken, my wife Elizabeth began to worry about me. 'Will you see the doctor if I make you an appointment?' she queried.

I told her I felt it was a waste of time, mine and the doctor's. The only thing that could really help was to bring Gary back and that was impossible, but I said I would go for her sake, if she was so worried.

When I saw the doctor I told him politely I felt that it was a waste of time. I didn't want to be on medication and I didn't want sleeping tablets. He was really good and said he would not have offered them anyway. We had a really long, helpful talk and he confirmed that I was suffering from normal grief, and I was to make another appointment to see him when the autopsy report arrived, and he could assess me then.

I had no shortage of people to talk to but I felt I needed more. I was really struggling. I contacted Cruse the bereavement people and was given an appointment for assessment. I hadn't contacted them lightly, for I was used to sorting out my problems myself, but all of this, Gary's death, all of the unanswered questions, it was all too much and I was way out of my depth. I received an appointment fairly quickly and attended their premises in Nottingham.

The lady I saw was very efficient and took all the details. She asked me if I had thought of taking my own life. I replied, 'Yes, I thought about it but I would never do it.' I explained I thought too much of my wife to leave her in that way, and also it would serve no purpose. I didn't believe that it would reunite me with Gary. However, you must understand I was so desperate to be with Gary. Had he returned from the grave and held out his hand for me to join him, I would have taken it without hesitation and followed him anywhere.

She explained she had lost her own son, so I knew she understood, but despite that there was no warmth, no compassion; it was as if it was an interview for a job. She told me it was too soon after my son's death, and I would get more from the counselling months down the line, and they would be in contact then. That was maybe how it worked, I didn't know. They were the experts, but I really felt that I needed help then.

You must remember I am not a religious person in any way, shape or form, so there was no comfort for me in the church. Now I know when some people have a traumatic experience in their life they turn to God and the church, and they find comfort there. If it works for them then that's wonderful, but it didn't work for me. The minister at my wife's church came to see me and, whilst his intentions were good and he was very caring, I told him tactfully after what had happened I couldn't listen to people telling me how wonderful God was. I didn't believe he even existed. Gary and I were not bad people, we didn't deserve this. If God had wanted to take Gary that would have been bad enough, but why did he have to take him in the circumstances that he did, leaving me with my burden of guilt and recrimination that I know will stay with me for the rest of my life?

Gary's key worker told me of an organisation called Spoda who helped with substance-related bereavement, but I decided not to call them. They probably wouldn't be of much help to me, or so I thought. Besides, I was already in touch with Cruse, so I left it at that. In the event, they called me. Andrea, Gary's key worker, had told them of my loss and given them my telephone number. I spoke to a lady called Dot. She arranged a time to visit me in my home and she was wonderful, warm and compassionate. She gave me a hug and, even though she had never met Gary, she made me feel we were both really important to her.

We arranged another meeting, again in my own home, and I felt so much better after talking to her. It didn't bring Gary back to me, of course, but it seemed to help me to bear the grief, if only for a short while. But, hey, I was going to take anything I could get if it helped me.

The days passed into weeks and Gary had received another letter from Europe Car, this time more official. I made enquiries and discovered that Gary had in fact hired a car and then passed it on to someone else. He had hired it, using his correct name and address and credit card, so he knew he would be getting the invoice. What was that all about? I was still really grief-stricken but was beginning to think a little more rationally.

I decided I would organise Gary's funeral. The least I could do was to try to give him a beautiful service. It wouldn't make any difference to the fact that he was gone, but at least it gave me something to focus on.

I chose the music. Gary hadn't really been into music in a big way so there was no obvious choice, so I picked three atmospheric tracks from Clannad, someone whose music we had played in the car when travelling away on our fishing adventures; the theme from Harry's Game to enter the chapel; "What Will I Do?" for the reflection, and "I Will Find You" to be played as everyone left the chapel. I also decided to get a photograph enlarged to place on the coffin at the service. Elizabeth found a fairly recent one of Gary with a very special catfish that he had caught, and I knew that he would have been pleased with it.

I also began to write a tribute that I would read out myself at the service or, at least, attempt it. I doubted I would manage to read it all the way through. I was still so emotional I would break down every day, sometimes several times a day, but at least I could try. I organised all the other details and arranged an appointment with the minister who was to take the service. As I have already mentioned, a lady called Caroline was in charge of the funeral arrangements and I felt that she really cared. She showed so much compassion and it really did help. I will always be so grateful to her.

It became apparent as I continued my investigations that Gary had indeed been in a mess. He owed thousands of pounds to various people, and had pawned the television, his smart phone, his tablet and who knows what else. He had returned his watch to the store and claimed a refund, and yet he still didn't have any money when he died and, remember, he was working so he had a reasonable income as well. Had it all indeed got too much for him? His debts, the state of the house, the problems with the drug dealer, the car he had rented which he knew would be another huge debt. Could he have taken his own life? I doubted it. He would surely, knowing Gary as I did, left me a note at least, or even a text. I doubted he would have killed himself without saying goodbye, as we were so very close.

Stranger things have happened, and who knows how he had felt at the end? Remember, I hadn't seen Gary for seven days because of his demands to borrow money. We had been in this position so many times before, but we had always resolved it and carried on, made it right, but this time there was no chance of that happening. He was gone. Had he killed himself? Depending on the results of the autopsy I might never find out the truth.

I had taken my eye off the ball, and I felt I had let him down. I hadn't been there for him when he needed me most. It all began to feel like it was more than I could possibly bear.

I had originally intended to cancel all the holidays we had pre-booked: three weeks in Thailand with Elizabeth, a fortnight in France with Gary, and a further fortnight in France with Elizabeth. I changed my mind. Elizabeth would come with me to France instead of Gary and the other holidays would be as arranged. I felt guilty for going and disrespectful to Gary but I just needed to be doing something, I needed to get away.

The days and nights passed so slowly I was in pieces. Gary's memories were everywhere. As I checked through his possessions at his home I found his personal things and it almost destroyed me every time I discovered them.

It was the small illogical things that seemed to upset me the most. On Christmas Eve I had taken Gary shopping for his groceries and he had chosen some own brand mince pies. I had discovered some Mr Kipling's on offer and he had bought these instead. At Gary's house, after his death, I found a bag of rubbish ready for the bin, and in it was all the Christmas paper from his presents and the empty boxes of Mr Kipling mince pies. It sounds silly but I was really emotional, and as I sat on the settee at Gary's house, feeling more than a little upset, I spotted Gary's canisters of E cig flavours. There was candy crush, cherry, coconut crush and several others. I picked them up and smelled them, all the individual smells I remembered each one as he had smoked them in his E cig. It was all too much and again the tears flooded down my face.

Do not weep for me,

I have no need of tears.

Instead let your heart be filled with joy

For the times that we were given.

Rejoice and remember me with love.

For while I am in your heart

And in your thoughts

I will live on

And I will be with you forever more.

David Michael Straw

CHAPTER 11

As I already said the days passed slowly, one merging into the other. I didn't feel like doing anything constructive although I knew I should have kept busy. I just sat about moping and I suppose feeling sorry for myself, but I just missed having Gary around so much that it actually hurt.

The funeral director, Caroline, contacted me to say that Gary was in the chapel of rest and I could visit him there. I went with Elizabeth and, on the way, called at the florist to buy a single red rose to place in his coffin. An elderly woman came in to the shop and, on seeing me buying the rose, said, 'I wish someone would buy me a red rose.'

'Not for the reason I am buying this one you wouldn't,' I told her.

At the chapel of rest Gary had been laid in the coffin dressed in a blue shroud, looking as though he was asleep. The tears just flooded down my face. Caroline was with me and held me as I cried for, as you can perhaps imagine, I was inconsolable.

I eventually turned away from Gary after saying my final goodbye and started to walk away, but I went back to him and stayed a while longer.

I said my goodbyes again and this time I didn't go back. It was so difficult, for I knew I would never see my son again.

All too soon it was the day of the funeral. I wasn't dreading it because, for just a little while, I could be close to Gary again. The funeral cars stopped outside my house, the house where Gary had grown up. It was an awful day, the rain was non-stop, but somehow it seemed so fitting as though all the angels in heaven were crying for Gary.

The cars set off in a slow procession, myself in the car behind the hearse. I just sat and stared at the coffin as we drove to the crematorium. I could barely believe my son Gary was in there even after all those weeks. I found it hard to comprehend he was actually dead.

When we arrived at the crematorium I was surprised at the number of people waiting there. A colleague had travelled down from the Lake District and some other friends had travelled all the way from Kent.

Caroline had said all along it was sensible to book a larger chapel. I had had my doubts but had bowed to her wisdom. Thankfully I had, for the chapel was almost full.

The service all went really well and so many people told me afterwards what a moving and beautiful service it was. I delivered my tribute to Gary and somehow I found the strength to read all of it. Although the service was emotional, from somewhere I felt an inner calm, a detachment almost from the reality of it all.

The service passed really quickly and afterwards I tried to speak to everyone who had attended, to thank them for their time and effort in being there. Most of the people returned to my wife's church for a cup of tea and a sandwich, after which it was home.

After all the preparation and emotion that had gone on before and during the funeral everything seemed almost like the quiet before the storm and I knew it was the beginning of the rest of my life without the physical presence of my son.

I also knew that life now was going to be totally different without my son being with me, but that, while I lived and breathed, my son's spirit would also live on. He would always be with me in my heart and would be constantly with me in my thoughts.

What follows is the tribute I wrote for my son.

This is a copy of the notes that I gave to the minister who conducted Gary's funeral.

Entrance music

Theme from Harry's Game / By Clannad.

A photograph of Gary with the biggest catfish that he caught in England was placed on Gary's coffin. The photograph was taken on 28th April 2014 shortly after 6.00am. This catfish is one of the biggest and most well-known fish in the UK and weighed a staggering 119 lbs.

Gary, although he doesn't look it, really was pleased with the capture.

The fish was released immediately after the photograph and is still swimming around its home in Oakwood Park, Norfolk, to this day.

Music for reflection

What Will I Do? / By Clannad.

The piece of music we are about to listen to is a track by Clannad and, although Gary never had any particular affinity with Clannad, it was their music that was frequently played on the car stereo as Gary and his Dad travelled together on their many fishing adventures.

So why this particular track now? Just listen to the words and I think you will understand.

Exit music

I Will Find You by Clannad.

This last piece of music is also by Clannad and again Gary had no particular affinity with it but the music is so haunting and atmospheric, and is a favourite of Gary's father. Again to understand his choice, listen to the words.

Post script

Even now, almost two years after Gary's death, if I listen to any of these tracks of music I am immediately transported back in time to the afternoon of Gary's funeral, and the sadness and utter desolation that I was feeling at that time. The music is to me very special and I still cannot listen to it without tears stinging my eyes and coursing down my cheeks. For that reason I no longer play these tracks, but for anyone who may be interested in listening to them they are on the CD Clannad- Best in a Lifetime.

This photograph used at Gary's funeral

Tribute to Gary 17.02.2016

May I welcome you all and thank you for taking the time and trouble to attend today. I have been overwhelmed by the sympathy and support shown to me by so many people. Before I begin this tribute to Gary may I just say that I have written it in the darkest and most desolate period of my life, and I have no idea of how these words will convey themselves to you. I have rewritten it so many times, and the words still seem so inadequate. Even my tears cannot express my feeling of loss.

Reading it will not be easy. I have cried so many tears I think there cannot possibly be any more, but still they come, and if I falter I ask for your understanding.

When Gary passed away it felt as though part of me had been taken with him. It was a relationship I had taken for granted; I thought Gary was always going to be part of my life. Only when he was taken from me so suddenly did I realise the richness and true meaning of the times we shared together. All I have left are the memories, and they are the most precious thing I possess.

There is a saying that you never know what you have until it's gone. This has never seemed so true. So many of us go through life wishing for so many things when, in reality, you already possess something far richer and meaningful than anything your wishes could bring you. The trick is to realise it.

Gary's death left a void so large inside me that no matter how long I live and no matter how many other things I try to put into that void I will never come close to filling it. And if you are hoping for this tribute to be warm and uplifting then I fear you will be disappointed.

For me there is no sunlit meadow, no chorus of bird song, no butterfly's flitting from flower to flower. Indeed the place in which I find myself is so deep and so dark I fear I may never walk in these places again. My emotions have gone from utter desolation and hopelessness to anger and resentment, and then back to despair. Not only have I lost my only son but also my best friend. Our lives were so entwined, we were so close. The pain I have experienced has been almost unbearable, and if these words sound deeply troubled it's probably because they are.

Gary was born on the 1St September 1975 in Derby city hospital at 1.30am, the first-born of two identical twins. The second-born, who was christened Michael, only managed to cling to life for a few days, and Gary became ever more precious.

Gary lived his very early years in Codnor before moving to Newthorpe in the spring of 1980. He attended the local infant, junior and finally comprehensive school before leaving to begin his working career.

He had several changes of career but the one he said he enjoyed the most was when he worked with me as a plumber and heating engineer. He remained living in Eastwood although he had several different homes before moving to Chilwell and finally Ilkeston, where he remained until his death in January of this year 2016.

Gary was not perfect; who is? But mostly he was the most kind, caring and loving son who would have literally given you his last Rolo. His love of nature and kindness to all animals was always evident.

We never really spoke of our feelings for each other but a few years ago now he sent me a father's day card which I came across after his death, when looking for some old photographs. The words on the card seemed so appropriate, and I would like to read them to you.

It's time I told you,

So I'm sending you this card,

To let you know just how I feel

As spoken words come hard.

You mean so very much to me,

And I don't often say

Just how much I love you

So I'm telling you today.

I know I'm not perfect,

Sometimes you have to moan,

Like when I'm in the shower too long,

Or maybe on the phone.

But you are mostly kind to me

And I do appreciate

All the things you do.

I think you're really great.

You've helped me on the right track

Whenever I did wrong.

Without a quibble you would help

You are so very strong.

I wouldn't want to change you,

Not at any cost.

What would I do without you?

I'd most certainly be lost.

Have a super day

To my lovely dad (Bonehead)

Love Gary x x x

As Gary became older we grew even closer, possibly because he never married and had children of his own. And apart from the many years we spent working together we spent many of our leisure hours together as well. From doing nothing special to the many happy times we spent fishing, not only in this country but also France and Spain. We mainly fished for catfish and when we fished together it would be as a team and we shared all our knowledge, and fished for each other. We usually caught more than anyone else on the lake and Gary would call us the "catmasters". He always called me Davey when we were fishing. I suppose it saved him shouting, 'Dad' across the lake.

If we weren't spending time together we would often be talking to each other on the telephone or sending texts, very often sharing our many private jokes. They weren't always funny but they were ours.

Recently, when looking through my texts, I came across one from Gary, and the first line read, *What's that got to do with owt?* It puzzled me until I opened it fully, and then I remembered. He had previously sent me a text saying, *ring u later mate*.

I texted him back saying, in fun, *What's with the mate bit? I'm your dad*. and he replied, *What's that got to do with owt? I'm still your friend, aren't I?*

Now those of you who knew Gary well knew that he wasn't without his troubles and sometimes if he felt he had let me down in some way he would say, 'One day I will make you proud of me.' To my eternal regret I never told him that I was already proud of him. Proud to have him stand alongside me as my son, proud to have shared forty years of my life with someone who was so kind and loving and, as Gary had stated in that text, I was his friend. Gary had no choice in the fact that I was his dad, but I was proud he had chosen me as his friend.

When I visited Gary in the chapel of rest he looked peaceful, and I stayed with him for a long time. I cried almost continuously but I poured my heart out to him, telling him all the things that I felt. Oh, how I wished I had told him those things when he was still alive. I finally said goodbye to him, turned my back, walked away and closed the door, knowing I would never see him again. But I couldn't do it, and I went back to Gary and said all of those things once more. I left him again and closed the door as I left. This time I didn't go back, although I wanted to so badly. It was the hardest thing I have ever had to do in all of my life. But I have another thing to do that will be even harder for me, and that is to spend the rest of my life without Gary at my side. Everywhere I go I have memories of him being there with me; my life seems so empty without him.

Our relationship was beyond priceless and I feel like the most precious and irreplaceable possession anyone could ever have has been taken from me. No words have ever been written that could portray that emotion.

Now I have put a few lines together in a poem, if you can describe it as such. When I had finished I decided it was far too dark to read out to you.

But I changed my mind and decided to read it anyway and you can make your own decision.

Somewhere in the darkest night

The angel of death begins his flight.

Death came unto me and beckoned me to go with him.

I at first refused and asked why have you come to me now at this time?

He replied, 'Though you have only lived a short life your time is now upon you'.

I asked could he not take someone older or more willing to go.

He replied, 'No, I have chosen you and you must come with me now.'

And so I must travel to a place far away,

But my spirit will always remain with you.

No more will I feel the warmth of the sun upon me,

Or feel the rain as it falls gently upon my face.

No more will I see the moon as it rises to its zenith in the heavens,

Or the myriad of the twinkling stars set into a black velvet sky.

No more will I gaze upon you,

Or hold you close, or speak with you of times we shared.

These things for me are now at an end

And I must travel to a place far away,

But my spirit will always

Remain with you.

(David Michael Straw)

Now I don't know what happens to someone when they die but when my own time comes, just perhaps I might travel to that same place far away, and just perhaps Gary will be waiting for me by the side of some beautiful lake set in that sunlit meadow and he will say, 'Come on, Davey. Where have you been? Let's get the Bivvy's up and then I'll put the kettle on.'

So until then, Gary, always remember I love you and miss you so much, and you did make me proud.

To quote the words from the piece of music we will listen to today: *What will I do without you? I don't know.*

Thank you for listening to me.

I leave a rose, a simple token.

Its beauty passing briefly by.

Hopes and dreams lie broken

But the memory lives. It will never die.

David Michael Straw

A single red rose that I placed in Gary's coffin
together with so many hopes and dreams.

CHAPTER 12

The time continued to pass slowly day by day. It was a really difficult time for me. People told me it was early days, and I was doing well, but I knew I had taken Gary's death really hard.

I was going to say I think it was the suddenness of it all, but I don't *think* it was. I *knew* it was. If Gary had been hospitalised for weeks or months on end with some terminal illness I could have coped much better. It would obviously have been horrendous, watching his life ebb away but, at the very least, I could perhaps have accepted what was to happen and prepare myself for it, or at least tried to.

As it was, there had been no warning, no thought of Gary's death. He had always been so healthy, fit and strong and so full of life.

I was forewarned I would probably never learn the actual day of his death or the exact circumstances surrounding it and I tortured myself with the thoughts of him dying alone. How long had he lain there? What were his last thoughts? When had the light faded from his eyes? When had his very last breath left his body? Questions I knew I would never have answers for, and questions I knew would torment me forever.

Apart from as a child when my grandfather passed away, I had never known or been involved in a sudden death. Whether it was because it was someone so close to me, my own son, I don't know, but I was finding it really hard to come to terms with.

I kept wishing to go back in time to, I don't know, perhaps be kinder to him, to have been more tolerant, or even just to have told him how much I loved him.

A friend of mine, some seventeen years before, had lost his daughter in a road accident, and obviously, I had felt sorrow and sympathy and I imagined, at the time, I knew how he must have felt. In reality I realise now that I had no comprehension of his feelings. Only when you experience it for yourself can you truly understand how devastating it really is.

The funeral director, Caroline, contacted me to say Gary's ashes were at the funeral parlour and could be collected whenever I was ready. I collected them the next day. They had been placed in a wooden casket with a brass plaque, and the first thought that struck me as I picked them up was how heavy they were. It was my intention to place them in the family grave, where only a few months before we had placed my mother's and my aunt's ashes. Gary had always been close to my mum and aunt. They had played such a large part in looking after him, both as a child and an adult, and I felt it was a comfort to me that he would be close to someone who loved him, instead of being alone.

For now I placed Gary in his old bedroom at our house, and it surprised me to realise what a comfort it was having him so close to me. As ridiculous as it may sound, I knew exactly where he was and that he was safe. There was also the matter of his home to deal with. The house he had lived in belonged to me, and it would have to be cleared and sold. Some people queried, 'Are you going to rent it?' but from my experience of finding Gary there, I just wanted it gone.

For now everything would have to be put on hold. Our holiday in Thailand was getting ever closer and everything would have to wait until we returned. I still hadn't heard from the coroner, almost eight weeks after the autopsy, and still didn't know what Gary had died of and, most importantly to me, whether he had taken his own life. I had rung them numerous times but was always told the same thing: 'When we have the information we will contact you.'

It was the day before we were due to leave for Thailand when we received a phone call. My wife Elizabeth answered it and told me it was for me: the coroner's office. With a pounding heart I took the phone. What would they tell me? The information I was about to be given was something that I was going to have to live with for the rest of my life, be it for the better or worse. I listened with hardly a breath as the lady on the other end of the phone told me, 'We have the results of your late son's autopsy.'

Gary had died of sepsis, blood poisoning that had started infections throughout his whole body. I realised this was hardly good news but I was so relieved. I knew it would not bring Gary back to me, but it meant he had not killed himself purposefully. He had not felt so desperate and hopeless he had felt the need to take his own life.

The holiday came and went as they do. It was enjoyable enough. Thailand is a beautiful place with a wonderful climate, although, if you don't like hot and humid, don't go to Thailand.

Gary was uppermost in my thoughts for the whole holiday. On the one hand I felt guilty for going on holiday so soon after his death but, on the other, I have always been pragmatic, so what was the point in sitting about moping. The whole holiday was very emotional for me. I missed the phone calls, the texts and the emails from Gary, but it was a relief to be somewhere neutral, somewhere without the memories of being there with him.

The return home was really hard. It felt really flat to be back after over three weeks away. There was, of course, no Gary to welcome me home and listen to my adventures. All my memories of him returned with a vengeance, but I just had to carry on and try to look forward to times when I hoped it would become easier. There was certainly plenty to keep me busy. Gary's home now had to be cleared and sold and, whilst I knew it had to be done, I wasn't looking forward to it. It was going to be emotional enough with the memories of him and all his possessions still being there. Added to this, all my mum's and aunt's things were still there, and I was born and raised as a child in that house; it had been bought by my grandfather in 1942, so seeing it sold was not going to be easy.

I also had to organise Gary's ashes being interred in the family grave. I had mixed feelings. On the one hand I was happy for him to be there with people that had loved him, but I was also finding a lot of comfort from him being where he was. I knew it was illogical, but I felt he was safe and still close to me, although I also felt it was perhaps a little macabre for wanting to keep his ashes in his old bedroom, now utilised as my study. As I said, mixed feelings.

Throughout all this time Dot from Spoda had continued to visit me. Not only did she give me someone to talk to, whom I felt understood, she also liaised with Gary's key worker, the police and the coroner's office providing practical help as well as emotional help.

Do not stand by my grave and mourn for me,

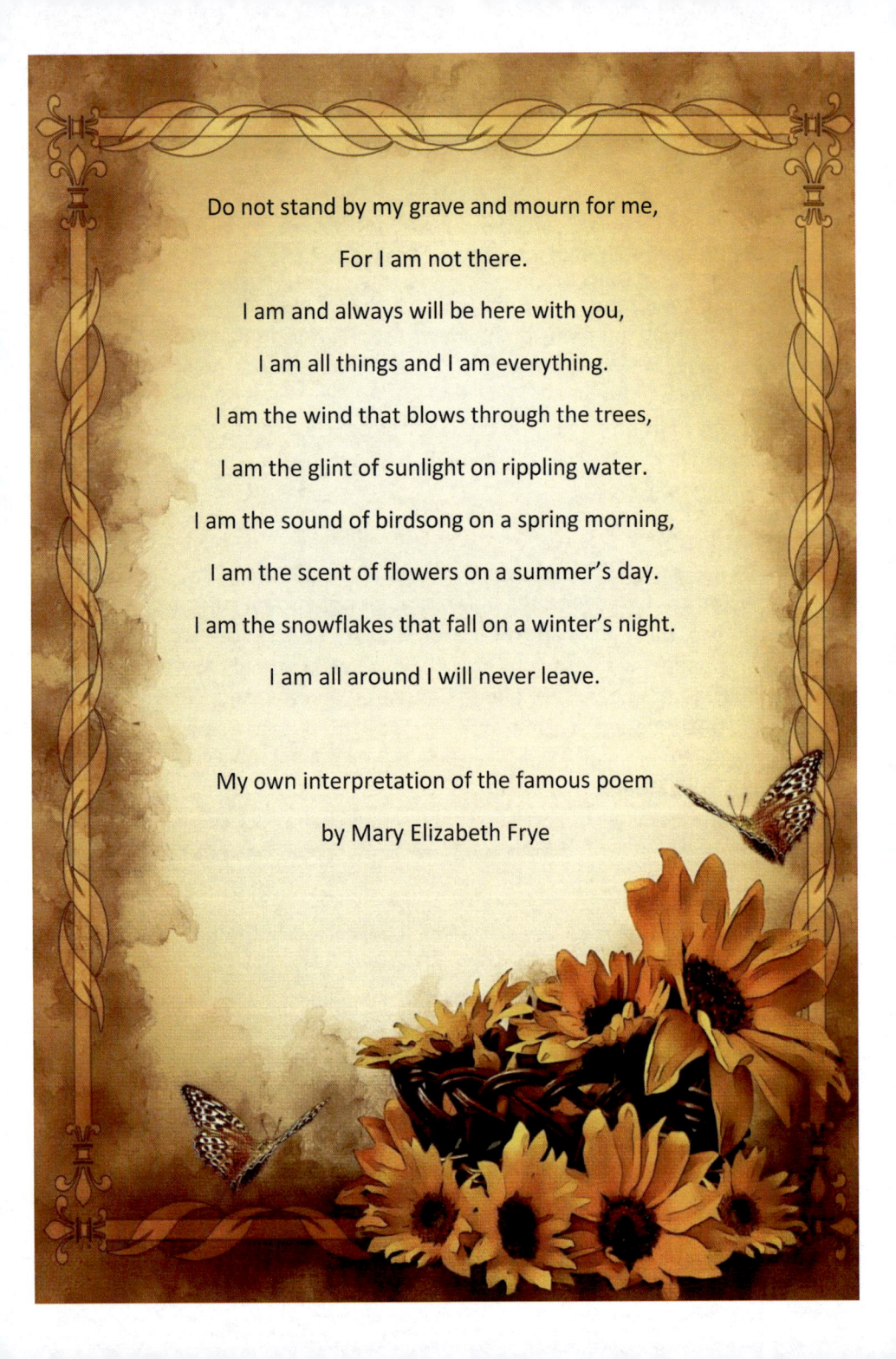

For I am not there.

I am and always will be here with you,

I am all things and I am everything.

I am the wind that blows through the trees,

I am the glint of sunlight on rippling water.

I am the sound of birdsong on a spring morning,

I am the scent of flowers on a summer's day.

I am the snowflakes that fall on a winter's night.

I am all around I will never leave.

My own interpretation of the famous poem
by Mary Elizabeth Frye

CHAPTER 13

I couldn't find any more excuses, couldn't put it off any longer, I needed to make a start on clearing Gary's home. The sooner I started, the sooner it would be finished, although I was still dreading it. A friend had offered to help me and I accepted gratefully; I really didn't want to begin the task alone.

The first part was reasonably easy. I organised a skip and all the furniture and old carpets were thrown into it. None of it was worth saving; it was old and worn out and, if I am honest, not very clean. But even though I knew it was only material possessions they held so many memories of times past. With the bulk of the basic contents sorted, it was becoming more difficult. I was down to the personal items belonging not only to Gary but also to my mum and aunt and even my grandparents. For now they were placed to one side. I was putting off the inevitable. I knew I couldn't save them all, for there was a house full, but it was going to be so very hard to throw away such personal possessions. I explained my feelings of disloyalty to my family to another friend, and told him it felt totally wrong to be discarding anything at all. They were, after all, the possessions my family had acquired over a lifetime, and they were in my care, and I was going to take them and throw them in a skip. He said I was wrong to think of it in that way. People had lived their lives and hopefully enjoyed their lives and they were just material things collected on the journey. It made me feel a little bit better thinking of it in that way, but it wasn't easy.

I had cleared some of the more perishable items belonging to Gary shortly after his death. I had emptied the fridge, thrown out all the old food items such as the milk etc. I had looked in the margarine tub and inside I could see the knife marks Gary had made the last time he used it. It seems a trivial thing looking back on it but at the time, to me, it was heart-breaking. I even had to empty the flask that Gary took to work, still half full of cold coffee, coffee that Gary had made and poured in there himself; should I save it? No, that was ridiculous, but even so there was a lump in my throat and a tear in my eye as I poured it down the sink and watched it slowly disappear.

Anything that was remotely of any value I boxed or bagged, things such as ornaments, tea sets, glasses, my mum and aunt's coats and dresses, they were all sent to charity shops or given to other deserving causes. Some items I just couldn't bear to part with, even though I knew I would struggle to find a place to keep them. One item in particular was the old family Christmas tree and the box of decorations. They had been pressed into service before I was born and for so many years after that almost up until very recent times. They had so many special memories, not only of Christmas itself, but a house full of relatives, all of whom had long since passed away.

There were boxes of my mum and aunt's Christmas and birthday cards dating back decades, letters from people no longer with us, even holiday postcards, some of them from myself to my mum and aunt sent when I was a child. They had saved them all. Documents and wills no longer valid, even paperwork from when my grandfather had purchased the house in 1942 for the sum of £250, accompanied by the solicitor's bill for £6/8 shillings. My grandparents had been renting the property before buying it, and I believe it was their first home in 1915 when they married, so it had been with the family for over a hundred years.

Boxes of photographs and family albums, all of these things I saved, too precious to throw away. But the thought did occur to me that someone, I don't know who, would one day have to make a decision as to their fate, someone who didn't know the people involved, and I realised these items so precious to me would be meaningless and worthless to them, but for now at least they were safe.

Gary didn't have a lot of his own possessions at the house. All his fishing equipment was at my house and, other than that, he had very little that he actually owned, most, if not all, of anything he owned of monetary value had been pawned or sold to obtain drugs.

I suppose most people who didn't know Gary personally would have thought of him as perhaps a waste of space or even a lowlife, but they couldn't have been more wrong. I know I am biased but he didn't have a malicious bone in his body, he would help anyone; he was kind and loving and loyal. He had the misfortune to be a drug addict, admittedly self-inflicted, but he had tried so many times in the past to break free. He had told me himself, on so many occasions, how he hated that side of his life, and he had been clear of drugs for long periods of time and been so proud of himself. Unfortunately, he was just not strong enough to break free for good. It's all too easy to be critical and to judge people, but I know how hard he had tried to be free. Perhaps by the grace of God go you and I.

Pretty much everything of Gary's I saved. I just couldn't throw anything of his away; it was just too emotional for me. It took a while but, eventually, the house was emptied and a final decision on its fate had to be decided. In fact it was an easy decision and one that I had made from day one – it was to be sold. At my age and with no children or grandchildren to leave it to, it made monitory sense to sell instead of renting it, but most importantly although, in one sense, it would be a sad day when it went, after so many years in the family, after my experience of finding Gary after his death I wanted it gone. Too many bad memories.

I contacted the estate agents and everything was put into motion and the house went on the market. I was persuaded to sell it with the latest marketing trend on the internet, the most efficient way to sell a house in modern times, or so I was told. I wouldn't have any estate agents cost, they would all be paid by the purchaser, but it sounded expensive to me on a house of that value. I was sceptical but they were the experts and so I went along with it. Time would tell who was right.

Of course over the several weeks it had taken to clear the house other things relevant to Gary had moved forward at a pace, and I continued to ride my roller coaster of emotions.

Drug induced living

81

82

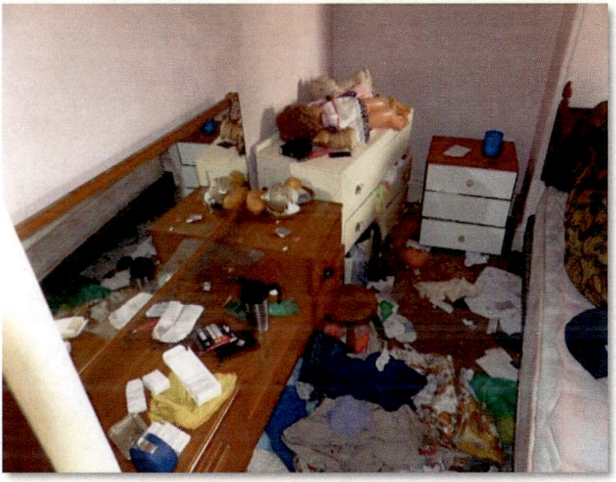

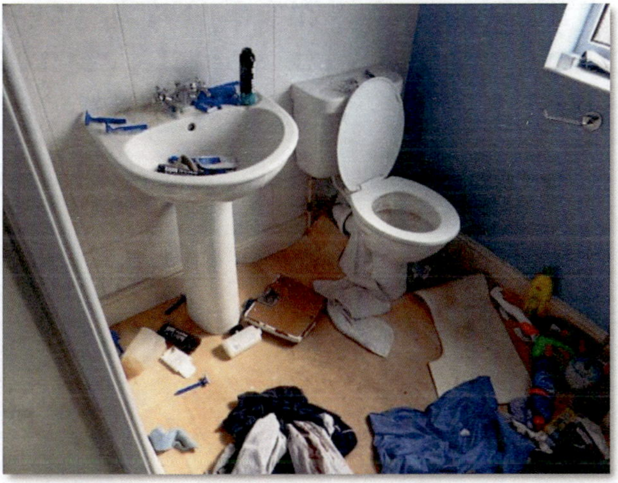

The ties that bound up in life are so strong

They cannot be broken, not even by death itself.

CHAPTER 14

When I returned from Thailand, amongst other mail, was the post mortem report. I had been warned it would make unpleasant reading and, whist it was certainly upsetting, my reaction was one of relief to see in black and white the facts to prove Gary had not killed himself purposely. The thought that Gary had been feeling so desperate to have taken his own life without being able to talk to me of his fears and despair would have been almost too much to bear. From the information I had acquired after Gary's death I knew things with him had been pretty desperate, and I also knew I hadn't spotted any outward signs and allowed things to spiral downhill. I also knew my feelings of guilt and responsibility would haunt me for the rest of my life. Too late now, obviously, but if only I had realised then, probably Gary's death could have been avoided.

The doctor had requested to see me when the post mortem results had arrived so I made an appointment and saw him a few days later. He expressed surprise that it had taken so long to receive it. He read it through patiently and then we had a conversation on our thoughts. From the information given in the report he explained that Gary's health must have been deteriorating for a while and at the time of his death, even if he had been able to access medical help, it was doubtful he could have been saved. I was somewhat shocked by this revelation. There had been no obvious signs. Gary had been fit and healthy and his normal self. The only thing that had been amiss was that just before Christmas Gary had complained of back ache and a pain in his legs. I ran him to his doctor's in the car because he had found it painful to walk. She had diagnosed Sciatica and given him a course of medication. He slowly improved and by the New Year was almost back to normal. Had it indeed been Sciatica or the first signs of his impending death? Had the doctor made a mistake and, if so, could his life have been saved? I was told the post mortem would not be able to give us any answers, and no matter what I did, it could never bring Gary back to me.

I decided not to take the matter any further. I had no proof of negligence in any case so it would be another unanswered question, but I still believe it was an opportunity that could have possibly saved Gary's life. The doctor continued to inform me all his major organs had been affected by the sepsis and he would almost certainly have suffered a heart attack. He also told me that, at the end, it would certainly have been over very quickly. He told me that if he had lingered he would have been in extreme pain and would definitely have sought help.

I had agonised over Gary's last moments and the thought of him dying alone with no one to help him, so to know he hadn't lain there hour upon hour in pain and mental anguish was at least some relief. The doctor then turned his attention to me and told me I was probably suffering from post-traumatic stress after finding Gary the way I had, and offered me a course of medication to help me. I didn't really want them but to refuse him after all his kindness and understanding seemed rather rude. I accepted them and completed the course. I didn't feel they helped me at all but who knows how I would have felt without them?

He rang me near the end of the course of tablets and I told him I was feeling pretty much okay, or at least as okay as I could be, because I was going away soon. It was almost time for the fishing holiday Gary and myself had booked. He offered me a repeat prescription in case I needed them whilst I was away. I thanked him politely but refused. He also suggested some counselling and gave me a telephone number I could call.

I had already begun seeing Cruse for counselling but didn't feel like it was helping me at all. The lady I had been involved with seemed very kind and understanding but for some reason I was getting nothing out of it; it just wasn't working for me. I remember on one occasion I had been early for an appointment and, as I waited in the car, I noticed there was a whippy ice cream van parked nearby. It was a really hot, sunny afternoon and I decided to buy one. Both myself and Gary loved whippy ice cream and when the opportunity arose we would always indulge. As I walked over to the ice cream van I was overcome with a feeling I can only describe as illogical, but nevertheless it overwhelmed me. If Gary couldn't enjoy an ice cream it wasn't right that I should. I turned around and walked back to my car, my eyes feeling more than a little moist.

I had already contacted the counselling service my doctor had suggested and they rang and gave me a date for my course to begin. I accepted but told them I was already seeing Cruse. They told me it was not recommended to see both of them concurrently, so I cancelled the rest of my appointments with Cruse and hoped I would get more out of my new counselling service. I had really surprised myself by seeking help in this way in the first place; it wasn't like me at all. I suppose it reflected how desperate and morose I really felt.

The Europe Car company had also sent further correspondence. Apparently, a traffic offence had been committed in Nottingham after Gary's death and a fine was due for payment as well as the original sum of money for the hire fee. A photograph of the incident was included and although the driver could not be identified in this instance, I was hopeful further C.C.T.V. footage could produce some new information as to his identity.

I passed all the new information on to the police who, by this time, had already recovered the car, which had been involved in an accident and suffered damage to a wheel and a front wing. The driver had not been apprehended. I was told the car had been subjected to D.N.A and finger printing but all to no avail. The car had been clean, whoever had driven it was obviously street wise. All we could hope for was that the C.C.T.V. would give us some new information as to the driver's identity.

The fishing holiday Gary and I had booked in France was getting ever closer and I had decided to go ahead, and go on the holiday with my wife, Elizabeth. I had no idea how traumatic I would find it, knowing I should have been sharing it with Gary.

The days continued to pass, nothing really eventful happening, now all we could do was wait for the inquest for which we still didn't have a date, but I knew I would learn very little from it anyway.

Whilst visiting Gary's old home I got talking to the neighbour, who told the police that he saw Gary on the 16th January, which was a Saturday. I had convinced myself he had been mistaken, everything pointed to Gary having died on the 13th or at the latest the 14th but he told me he had actually spoken to Gary face to face. I didn't know what to think. Could he have been mistaken? Was it the week before perhaps? But he was adamant he was correct, so this was yet another question that we would probably never find the answer to.

Dot still continued to visit me and I actually looked forward to her visits; she was someone who I could talk to about Gary, and how I was feeling. Dot had never met Gary but it felt as though she had known him, and really understood what I was feeling.

The police contacted me to say that the C.C.T.V. checks had not shed any light on who was driving the car that Gary had hired and, with the forensic checks having given us no clues, it looked as if there was no way the case was going to progress any further, and yet another unanswered question was added to the ever growing list of things I would never know.

What we cannot change

We must endure.

CHAPTER 15

The time for the fishing holiday in France arrived. It had been booked probably eight or nine months earlier. I felt a little guilty and disloyal to Gary for planning to go but, equally, it would serve no purpose to cancel it. I couldn't bring him back and it was pointless moping about the house and, hopefully, the break would be beneficial to myself and Elizabeth.

As I packed all the equipment into the trailer I stored all of Gary's gear into the garage. Everything was how he had left it, his bivvy neatly packed into its bag, his bed chair with his blanket inside of it and, most upsetting of all, his rods.

For his birthday the previous year he had been given three rod sleeves. His cat-fishing rods were his pride and joy and he had cleaned and polished them and put them into his new sleeves all ready for the new season to begin in spring. As I unzipped the sleeves and gazed at his rods I felt a tear in my eye, because now, for Gary, that new season would never arrive.

Gary and I loved our fishing sessions together. It was so much more than just catching fish: the closeness with nature, the relaxing with no outside pressure and the quality time we spent together.

After Gary's death many of my friends had told me that when things are a little bit more settled we would organise some fishing trips together. I never said anything to them, it sounded so ungrateful of their offer, but I didn't want to go with my friends, I wanted to be with Gary. I know it was impossible, but it was just the way I felt.

Elizabeth and I arrived at the lake in France and the holiday went well, apart from the weather. It was apparently the worst and wettest weather for one hundred years. How typical that it had to happen while I was over there. Gary was obviously constantly in my thoughts but strangely enough I didn't find it emotional. I think it was the fact that he and I hadn't been there together.

Later in the year I returned to France to spend two weeks on another lake where Gary and I had fished several times. I found the time there quite upsetting and emotional, with so many memories: the trees we had sat under to get shade from the sun, the bush by the side of the lake where I fell off my bicycle and got stuck, my bottom in the water. Gary was trying to pull me out but we couldn't move for laughing.

Whilst on my first holiday I had received a phone call telling me the date for the inquest, 17th August. I had mixed feelings about the inquest. I still hoped to gain some new information, although I doubted it, but I also knew that when it was over everything would be done and dusted, so to speak, and all I could do then was get on with my life, welcome of course, but I would have no direct contact with Gary anymore. It may sound ridiculous but while I was dealing with matters relating to him I could still feel a closeness between us.

Dot warned me that I would probably find the inquest deeply upsetting. She explained it would bring everything back. I told her that no, it wouldn't, because everything had never gone away; all my memories were still sharp and vivid, memories set in technicolour.

The house was still up for sale. I had been given quite a few offers, but I felt they were all derisory. It wasn't so much the money, it was the fact that the house had been in the family for so long, and my mum and her sister had lived there all their lives. I just felt they were an insult to their memory, and declined them all.

When I returned from the holiday in France I packed all his equipment into my trailer where it was stored. As I picked up his bed chair I noticed he still had his storage bag strapped to it, only small but ideal to keep your keys and other small items in. I looked inside and found one of his E cig refills with a small amount of liquid still inside it. As I unscrewed the top I read the label: 'Granny Smith'. I smelt the liquid and was instantly transported back to the time we had last cat-fished together. We were standing together beside a favourite lake of ours in Norfolk. I commented to him as he took a puff on his E cig, 'That's a strange smell. What flavour have we got this time?'

'Granny Smith' he replied.

'What! I bet that's disgusting'.

He laughed out loud and replied, 'No it's really nice'.

As I held the refill tightly in my hand I sat in my drive and the tears flowed unashamedly down my face.

The days continued to merge into weeks as the time passed. Obvious though it sounds, the time since I had seen or spoken to my son lengthened and it saddened me. It may seem to anyone reading this that I am a bit of a drama queen, but you have to remember, not only was he my son, he was my friend. We had shared so many special times together, we had also shared hard and difficult time together and this alone brings people closer.

I had wondered whether he would live or die for weeks on end after he was born prematurely. He only weighed three pounds at birth. I stood and watched as he lay in his incubator at the hospital, his little hands so tiny, and his fingers barely big enough as he grasped your own finger when touching him. We watched as his twin brother died after forty hours, hoping and praying Gary would be strong enough to survive. We took him home after six weeks, nursed him as he grew into a strong and healthy child.

I brought him up as a single parent from the age of five until he was fourteen. If he grazed his knee I cleaned him up and stuck a plaster on it. I dried his tears and gave him a cuddle and a kiss. As he grew up we shared so much of our time together, we looked out for each other. If you couple all this with the fact that I felt responsible for his death, I felt so guilty I had let him down, and not been there when he needed me the most.

If you have ever lost a child of your own, and I wouldn't wish that fate on anyone, believe me, perhaps you can understand why I had taken Gary's death so badly. Not only did I miss him so much, it changed my whole outlook on life. Before his death I had always looked forward to what the future may bring. Now I found myself looking back, remembering happier times. Of course I still have Elizabeth to share my life with. She is, and always will be, very important to me, but it is a totally different relationship to the one you share with your child.

I had worked hard all of my life, saved some money, and built my own property, all things that you hope your children would benefit from. Now there is nobody to leave it to. If anything happens to Elizabeth, if she goes before me, there will be nobody left, no one to shed a tear at my passing. All those things you worked for as a young man, all those dreams, all those hopes now seem so pointless. Growing old with no family around you suddenly becomes very frightening.

I realise I am wallowing in self-pity but I stated at the beginning I would write this with honesty and sincerity, and all I am doing is putting my thoughts to paper.

To wish you here, it will not succeed,

For believe me I have tried,

Nor to shed a tear in times of need,

For believe me I have cried.

David Michael Straw

CHAPTER 16

The day of the inquest arrived; all the arrangements had been made. Dot was coming over to our house and travelling to the coroner's office in my car with Elizabeth and myself. Andrea, Gary's key worker was to meet us there. The policeman who had originally responded to my 999 call was also to attend.

Gary's biological mum had been informed of the date. I had also offered transport to enable her to attend, but she had been non-committal as to her intentions. In the event she didn't attend or even telephone afterwards as to the resulting verdict, something that I found unbelievable, considering she was his mum.

Everything went well, the coroner was respectful and professional but I was as wise after the verdict as I was before it. No light was shone upon the time of death or any other details for that matter, the coroner explained that when someone dies alone it is very difficult to pinpoint details.

A full word-for-word transcript follows.

That was it then, just the sale of the house to go through and everything was final and complete, something I guess most people would be thankful for. As for myself, yes, it would be good for everything to be settled, but even so, a part of me would be a little sad. It was like bringing a chapter of my life to a close.

It had been and still was a harrowing and emotional chapter but, as I told my counselling therapist, if she could have given me a tablet to erase all the memories, horrific as they were, I wouldn't have taken it. I needed all those memories to be sharp and clear in my mind, as I expected they would be until my dying day. The emotions and memories would never leave me.

My counselling had finished. Had it helped? I honestly don't know. I had poured out all my feelings, all my emotions, but I did that every day to myself anyway, but overall I do think it was a worthwhile experience.

The offers on the house still came but they were still derisory. People are not stupid; the high fee on a property of that value was just being deducted from their offer. I decided to take it out of the hands of the original estate agents and sell it by more conventional means. Would it pay off? Time would tell.

Record of Inquest

Following an investigation commenced on the 21st day of January 2016
And Inquest opened on the 21st day of January 2016;
At an inquest hearing at Derby Coroner's Court on the 18th day of August 2016 heard before Miss Louise Pinder Assistant Coroner in the coroner's area for Derby & Derbyshire Coroner's Area, the following findings and determinations were made:

1. Name of Deceased (if known)

    Gary David STRAW

2. Medical cause of death
    - 1a Septic Shock
    - b   Multiple Visceral Infarction and Microabscess Formation
    - c   Intra-venous Drug Abuse
    - II

3. How, when and where, and for investigations where section 5(2) of the Coroners and Justice Act 2009 applies, in what circumstances the deceased came by his or her death

    Gary Shaw was found deceased at his home on 18th January 2016. He had a long documented history of illicit drug abuse. Post Mortem toxicology analysis did not reveal acute drug toxicity but the changes observed during the post mortem examination were associated with a general pattern of abuse over a number of years.
    Recent injection sites were noted in both groins.

4. Conclusion of the Coroner as to the death

    Drug related death.

5. Further particulars required by the Births and Death Registration Act 1953 to be registered concerning the death

(a) Date and place of birth 1 September 1975	Derby
(b) Name and Surname of deceased Gary David STRAW	
(c) Sex Male	(d) Maiden surname of woman who has married
(e) Date and place of death Eighteenth January 2016 30 Bloomsgrove Road, Ilkeston	
(f) Occupation and usual address Plumbing and Heating Engineer 30 Bloomsgrove Road, Ilkeston	

Signature of Assistant Coroner .... Miss Louise Pinder

TRANSCRIPT OF EVIDENCE HEARD AT THE INQUEST INTO THE DEATH OF GARY DAVID STRAW HELD AT DERBY ON THE 21ST JANUARY 2016 AND BY ADJOURNMENT ON THE 18TH AUGUST 2016 BY MISS LOUISE PINDER H.M. ASSISTANT CORONER FOR DERBY AND DERBYSHIRE

Date 20th January 2016

MISS MELANIE THEAKSTONE upon her Oath states:-

I am employed as a Coroner's Officer by HM Coroner for Derby and Derbyshire. On the 20th January 2016 I took details from David Michael Straw who is the father of Gary David Straw. David Michael Straw confirmed that the deceased's full name was Gary David Straw whose date of birth was the 1st September 1975. Mr Straw was born in Derby. The last occupation was as a Plumbing and Heating Engineer and the home address of the deceased was 30 Bloomsgrove Road, Ilkeston. Mr Straw was single. Mr Straw was pronounced dead on the 18th January 2016 at his home address of 30 Bloomsgrove Road, Ilkeston.

Date 18th August 2016

Legal Representation

Exhibits

Post Mortem Examination Report and Toxicology Report admitted under the Coroners rules.

Cor. Good afternoon everybody. This is the resumed Inquest touching the death of Gary David Straw. This Inquest was formally opened on the 21st January of this year; there was a short hearing which I know none of the family members came to, but we had to have a preliminary hearing in Court, in the very early stages of this investigation so that we could deal with a number of preliminary matters. We do not ask the family to come to that initial hearing because we are aware that you have enough to be dealing with in those early stages, and there is no evidence of any merit heard during the course of the preliminary hearing, but we have to have that hearing to establish the identity of the deceased and a number of other matters so that we can allow the family to go ahead with the funeral. So in fact it was my colleague Dr Hunter, who was in Court on that occasion. He opened the Inquest and then he promptly adjourned the Inquest so that the investigation could be completed. My name is Louise Pinder and I am one of the other Coroner's here in Derby. I became involved in the investigation into Gary's death only very recently, in fact the matter was set down for Inquest. A decision was made that PC Slee would be called to give evidence and the other witnesses, Dr Hitchcock and Dr Morley who were giving evidence with regards to the medical history here, the medical cause of death, a decision was made that their statements could be relied on rather than calling them to give evidence, and it was only within the last few days that this matter was then put before me. But is has been investigated: Miss Theakstone who is a Coroner's Officer here in Derby, she has been involved in the investigation, has been concluding the investigation. I understand, Mr Straw, she may have been in touch with you.

Mr Straw.   Is this Melanie?

Cor.   This is Melanie, yes.

Mr Straw.   Yes.

Cor.   I think she has been speaking to you hasn't she?

Mr Straw.   Yes.

Cor.   And she wrote to you and invited you to come to the inquest here today and obviously you are here. So, Mr Straw, I am assuming you are Mr Straw, father of Gary?

Mr Straw.   I am, yes.

Cor.   Can I just ask you who else you have got with you here today?

Mr Straw.   This is Dot, this is my wife, Elizabeth, Gary's stepmum, and this is Andrea, she was Gary's Social Care Worker.

Cor.   Oh, hello. Thank you all for coming. It is quite unusual that we have professionals as well as family in Court unless they have been called. And it is very nice to see you, thank you very much for coming in supporting the family. I don't know how much you understand about what we need today. I have to say that most people who come to the Coroner's Court come really not understanding particularly what the process it.

Mr Straw.   No, I've never been to an Inquest before, this is the first time.

Cor.   Well let me just explain it to you then, and I will try not to blind you with science, or blind you with law as it were, but I will explain in very brief terms what we need to do today. Gary's death was reported to us by both the Constabulary and also by East Midlands Ambulance Service, and that is normal, so when somebody dies suddenly and unexpectedly in the community, regardless of the medical cause of death, the Police attend, and obviously PC Slee attended, and has produced a report for my benefit, and also the East Midlands Ambulance Service are the ones that call the Police.

Mr Straw.   They did actually, yes.

Cor.   So when the emergency call goes through then obviously they despatch an ambulance but if then the death is certified, and the cause of death is not immediately understood, the death being unexpected and sudden, then the Police become involved. Now PC Slee will, I am sure, have told you and will confirm again today that part of what they are looking at is whether there are any suspicious circumstances. But they reported to us fairly early on in the process that they didn't believe that there were suspicious circumstances but they continue to investigate, produce a report and then ultimately very often they are asked to attend the Coroner's Inquest as Coroner's Officers, knowing that there will need to be an Inquest in due course, and this is why PC Slee is here. So, some family members get quite hot under the collar about the fact that there are Police Officers in Court; it doesn't imply that there is anything suspicious or untoward going on. They are the ones on the ground, is it were, who carry out our investigations in these circumstances, so it is important for me to hear evidence from PC Slee about that although, as I have mentioned he has already prepared a very detailed report for me for which I am grateful. The first part of the process as far as we are concerned, then is attempting to establish the medical cause of death. Now we do that by instructing one of our independent Pathologists, and on this occasion it was Dr Hitchcock who has worked with this Service for very many years. He doesn't attend the scene ordinarily. Very rarely would he attend the scene, we rely on the information that the Police and the Ambulance Service provide to us, we pass that on to Dr Hitchcock. Dr Hitchcock then carries out his examination, that is at the hospital in Derby and he is looking for the medical cause of death, and he has reported to me what that is, and you are aware of that I think.

Mr Straw.   Yes.

Cor.   Now once Dr Hitchcock had contacted us in those very early states, he was already suggesting to us that Gary's death was related to the history that had been presented to us that he had taken illicit drugs in the past, and he involved a Toxicologist to see whether or not actually Gary had died as a result of an overdose or toxicity in relation to those drugs, but he himself, Dr Hitchcock, carried out what we describe as a routine post mortem examination to see whether there were any pathological changes that would explain how it was that Gary came by his death.

And that question of 'how' is very important because the legislation places on me an obligation to determine, during the course of the investigation, and to confirm at the Inquest here today, the answer to a number of legal questions, the most important in this case being how it was that Gary came by his death. The legal questions are: who the deceased was, where, when and how he came by his death and that is laid down in the 2009 Act. But we pretty quickly knew who Gary was because there was a formal identification, we knew where he died, that was his home, there were some discussions we had today about exactly when that happened, but the key question really for me is how he died. It included the medical cause of death so I have to look at events leading up to his death and ultimately at the end of this inquest today I have to determine that question of how and translate it into a, what we used to call a verdict, but in fact the terminology has changed and it is now called a formal conclusion, but it is the same thing. So a formal conclusion as to how it was that Gary died, and there are a number of short form conclusions available to me, such as accidental death, there is a new short form conclusion that we are encouraged to return if we thing it is a drug-related death, partly for statistical purposes, it is important that the information is collated properly. And there are other options available to me as well. So that is what I am required to do. Now the point of all this from your perspective: well, I know that you have raised some questions, and I have seen a couple of the questions that you have raised in the letter that you kindly wrote to Melanie which she put before me, and obviously we will endeavour, if we can, to answer those questions here today. Above and beyond that, the purpose of the exercise from your perspective, and you as a family are at the heart of this, is to try and understand, perhaps from a slightly different perspective, but of course the question of how is as important to you as it is to me in a legal context to you as a family. So I hope when you leave here today you may have a clearer understanding of how it was that Gary died, and if that is the case then of course PC Slee and I have done our jobs properly. So that is what I hope. But just to manage your expectations, we can't always answer all of the questions.

Mr Straw. Well I have been told not to, you know, be too expectant of the result, so, you know, I am prepared for whatever.

Cor. Ok. But we are here to try and help.

Mr Straw. Yes.

Cor. But I mean things, for example, like giving a precise time of death, I will explain this in more detail in due course, is sometimes difficult because the science isn't there and it is all very well me plucking a time out of the air, but if you are looking for something more precise than that...

Mr Straw. There are just one or two, sort of, contradictory details...

Cor. Well I think we can work through that here today, can't we, and hopefully between PC Slee and myself we can help to answer some of the questions that you have.

Mr Straw. Thank you.

Cor. So that's the purpose of the exercise. Now once the inquest is concluded, assuming it is concluded here today, then the next stage is for me to organise for registration of Gary's death and the only way that we can do that is by having the Inquest concluded, confirming the medical cause of death and confirming how it was that Gary died, and then that information is all passed on by me to the Registrar and you will then get a full and final death certificate produced by the Registrar, but we can talk about that later on. So let me just start to go through the evidence with you then. If we go back right to the beginning, I was told that the East Midlands Ambulance Service and the Derbyshire Constabulary had reported his death and I see from the file that I have in front of me that we have the paperwork on file to support that. So the diagnosis of death form, which is probably not the best name for it, but it says what it does, is a form produced by the East Midlands Ambulance Service because Paramedics now are entitled to certify death. In the old days, and I can't remember just when the legislation changed, but it had to be a Doctor, and then they changed the rules and said that actually Paramedics were entitled to certify death. So when the Paramedics arrived...

Mr Straw. I believe they had to contact a Doctor, I think they said that he wouldn't necessarily attend, and I can't remember to be honest.

Cor. Yes well the Doctor would sometimes attend and that would be arranged by the Police but the actual certification of Gary's death was done on this occasion by a Paramedic, which was perfectly appropriate. So you will recall that the Paramedics attended. They say that the call was received by them at 15:02 on the 18th January.

Mr Straw.   Yes.

Cor.   They arrived on scene at 15:04 so they were extremely prompt…

Mr Straw.   Yes, to be honest I have no idea of the time lapse.

Cor.   I can imagine. Time takes on a completely different feeling doesn't it.

Mr Straw.   My impression was that they did arrive very quickly.

Cor.   They very quickly determined that Gary had very sadly died and they had completed the paperwork to say that he was certified deceased, and I am just looking for the time, at 15:12, and that was by Susie Ghee and it was witnessed by Rachel Taylor, who I assume are the two Paramedics.

Mrs Straw.   Well I don't know their names, to be honest, but yes, the two young ladies who attended.

Cor.   And they have indicated on the form that they sent to us that they were organising that the Police attend the scene.

Mr Straw.   Yes, they rang. I made the initial 999 call, and other than that everything was dealt with by the professional bodies.

Cor.   They confirmed that the information that they had been given was that the patient was last seen by father about a week ago, today the patient's father found him unresponsive, on the bed upstairs. Dad states that he texted the patient over the last couple of days and had no response. They carried out their own examination of Gary; they said that there were no breathing signs, that he was cold and that rigor mortis was present, and that the property was unkempt and that there were needles and syringes around the house. The information presented to them was that he was known to take drugs. They confirm that there was no, what they call bystander CPR, in other words that no CPR had been carried out because there were no signs of life.

Mr Straw.   No.

Cor.   And they go on to say that there were no obvious signs of death, and it was on that basis that they certified his death, as I say at 15:12. So that is the information we have from the Ambulance Service. I am not going to go into a lot of detail about the information we got from the Constabulary because of course we have got the Police Officer here, but we had a detailed Form 38, which is the form that we would expect to receive from the Police, which contained not only Gary's personal detail, information about when the Police attended, the fact that the Paramedics attended, but also some information about the circumstances, and I note in that Form 38 that the Police had understood that he was a known IV drug abuser and that he had been known to take heroin and cocaine in the past. The reason I mention that is because that information that we received in those early stages we passed on to our Consultant Pathologist so that the examination he carried out was in that context. Remember that the Pathologist, the same with the Police, the pathologist and us in the Coroner's service, we keep a very open mind in those early stages so it is important that we have as much information as we can about the circumstances of somebody's death, but we don't restrict our investigations and our enquiries to just that, we look at everything to try to determine how it was that he died. So Dr Hitchcock, I have mentioned already, a very experienced Pathologist, we asked him to carry out an examination which he did on the 20th January. That was done at the Royal Derby Hospital. I am not going to go through the report in any great detail, but what I want to refer you to is the fact that there were some external marks that I think are important…

Mr Straw. I did receive a full post mortem report which I read, they warned me that it wouldn't be pleasant reading, but I did receive it and, you know, read it and understand it.

Cor. Well in that case I am not going to go through it in any detail but you will recall that. I think it is important for me to note for the record, that there were signs of injection sites, externally, and I think the Police Doctor who attended had already confirmed that, but Dr Hitchcock saw that for himself. Dr Hitchcock carried out what we call a routine post mortem examination but it did include histology, and histology is where Dr Hitchcock has taken very small samples of lung, spleen, kidney and heart and also bone marrow and liver. Postage stamp sized samples but the point of that is that there is a certain amount that he can see during the course of the examination naked eye, but he very often will need to look through the microscope to see if there are any changes that are more subtle, so he carried out that histology analysis and he has explained in his report what he found, and there were some significant findings. And in addition to that he requested a toxicology analysis, which is to look at a sample of blood, and also urine in this case, to see if there was anything else going on behind the scenes. We very often take toxicology anyway, but with somebody who had a history such as Gary's, obviously what we want to look at is to see whether or not there were any drugs in his system that might account for his death. Now that toxicology analysis was carried out by Dr Morley, Dr Steven Morley, who is a Forensic Consultant Chemical Pathologist and a Forensic Toxicologist. He is based at the hospital in Leicester, we use the service in Leicester to carry out the toxicology analysis, and he screens initially for just about everything and anything, in terms of illicit drugs, prescription drugs, looking for ethanol – alcohol to you and I, and then once he finds certain things in the system he then carries out tests to see whether or not it is at overdose level or within therapeutic range. Again I am not going to go through the report in any great detail but his conclusions were that he did find some... he found no ethanol, so no alcohol.

Mr Straw.   No.

Cor.   But he did find some drugs within Gary's system but they were not at toxic levels.

Mr Straw.   No.

Cor.   So Gary did not die as a result, the Pathologist and Toxicologist are saying, as a result of toxicity or an overdose. There is a bit of distinction between the two, so an overdose, with a lot of drugs the Toxicologist would be able to say to us whether or not it falls within lethal range, and some of the drugs that were found in Gary's system fell within therapeutic range, some did fall within that higher range, but overall the feeling was that he hadn't died directly as a result of those drugs that he had taken, and the Pathologist, who has relied obviously in part on his own findings, and also in part on Dr Morley's findings, has concluded that actually Gary died as a result of changes that had come about as a result of long term drug abuse rather than toxic overdose in relation to those drugs on that particular day. You will remember that he has given the medical cause of death, you may not remember but I shall tell you, 1(a) Septic Shock.

Mr Straw.   Yes.

Cor.   He says that was due to 1(b) Multiple Visceral Infarction and Micro Abscess Formation, and 1(c) Intravenous Drug Abuse. So you sort of read the cause of death the other way round – what he is saying it that the start of all this is that Gary was an intravenous drug user, that led to the changes he saw, so the visceral infarction and the micro abscesses, and he has gone through that in some detail in this report, so there were longstanding changes that had occurred as a result of IV drug use, but what he is saying is that the terminal event, the reason that Gary died when he did was as a result of septic shock linked to that.

Mr Straw.   Yes.

Cor.   He has said, Dr Hitchcock in his comments section, that all the pathological features that he saw at post mortem examination, and he has discussed them in his report, he says are a likely consequence of repeated intravenous drug abuse, with evidence of recent injection sites in both groins. And you will remember that the histology examination in his report he has noted that there were changes, infarct changes within the spleen, both the kidneys and the heart, and in fact the heart also showed changes of an acute, so relatively recent, myocardial infarction, which is a heart attack to you and I.

Mr Straw.   Yes.

Cor.   He is saying that that is also related to the intravenous drug use, so unfortunately because of long-standing intravenous drug use, there was significant damage to his spleen, his kidneys and his heart, and that led to the development ultimately of septic shock.

Mr Straw.   So, to understand that correctly, I know you have said it was long term, but I understood it as he had possibly injected himself, got an infection, and it all stemmed from that one infection, but what you're saying is that it had built up over a long period, and it wasn't a single infection that he got in one injection.

Cor.   That is exactly right. It is clear that he had got septic shock which is an infection, but what Dr Hitchcock is saying is that there were multiple sources for that infection, but all relating to the fact that he had injected himself over a long period of time. So I think your interpretation is correct, that it is not one single event.

Mr Straw.   No, I just assumed that he'd just, for whatever reason, got a dirty needle, or whatever, and that had given him the infection and that was why he has died. It had been a single incident in a long line of incidents, but obviously that's not correct.

Cor.   No, Dr Hitchcock is saying that it is a combination of all these other things and it all led to the development of septic shock. What we can't say of course is what was the tipping point.

Mr Straw.   No.

Cor.   Because clearly Gary had lived for many years with a number of the changes that we saw at the post mortem because they are not things that all happen very quickly or very recently. It is difficult for us to identify then why it was that six months ago he was well and suddenly now he's become very unwell. I have to say that it is very difficult in all sorts of different scenarios to identify what the tipping point for people is but the reality is as we all, regardless of our backgrounds, if we become unwell, we have a reserve, the human body is designed in such a way that we fight infection, for example, we have a certain reserve, all of us, in that and the one day, you know, the balance is tipped, there is suddenly nothing left if you like in the tank to fight that infection and once the balance is tipped it is very difficult then sometimes to tip the balance back. The other point of course is that it is impossible for me to say whether or not if he had taken himself to the hospital and obtained some medical intervention, whether or not he would have survived.

Mr Straw. Well I did speak to someone with medical knowledge and they told me that a heart attack would have been so painful that he would have sought help, he wouldn't have laid there with, so in his opinion it would have happened very quickly.

Cor. Was that the GP?

Mr Straw. Yes.

Cor. Yes, the answer to all of that is that of course because we don't know what happened in his final hours, it is difficult to know whether or not Gary did become unwell, the other scenario of course is that if he had taken drugs which we know he had, that may have masked a lot of the symptoms.

Mr Straw. It was fairly low levels though, I believe.

Cor. Well it was very difficult, because there were some levels, but of course the difficulty that we have is that it is almost impossible to do a back calculation, because we don't know when he died, we only know when he was found, it is quite difficult for us to interpret, I mean it is difficult for us anyway to interpret the drug levels, but it is quite difficult to know that. I suspect, and I put it no more highly than this, that Gary had taken some illicit drugs, which he had done many, many times in the past. It may well have disguised, or in fact even have helped him to deal with the symptoms that he would have had because, there is no doubt in my mind that he would have felt unwell.

Mr Straw. Yes.

Cor. He may not have understood why he was feeling unwell; in fact I think it is extremely likely that he wouldn't have understood that. But it may well have masked some of those symptoms and, I don't know what his personality was, whether or not he would have wanted to have sought medical attention, but if he would have done ordinarily and he didn't on this occasion it may be just that he didn't appreciate quite how unwell he was.

Mr Straw. No.

Cor. And as I say, at some point the balance was tipped suddenly he wasn't able to fight the infection, septic shock then set in.

Mr Straw. Apparently it can occur even just over a few hours, I was told. As quickly as that, not necessarily days, it can literally...

Cor. Except I think the underlying changes are relatively chronic, ongoing changes, but I agree in terms of the septic shock that can happen very, very quickly indeed. So we will never know whether or not he was aware as to the fact that he was ill, and if he was aware I suspect he didn't realise quite how unwell he was. But if he had gone to hospital and sought medical attention, it may be of course that they would have been able to treat him – we will never know that.

Mr Straw. No, I mean the GP said that it was likely even if he'd had him in hospital, or that sort of situation, that it would have been extremely doubtful that he would have survived with the severity of his infection on his body.

Cor. Was it Dr Davis that you spoke to?

Mr Straw. No, Dr Exley, he's not Gary's GP, he was my GP.

Cor. Oh I see. Well we had a report from Dr Davis at The Old Station Surgery and I just wanted to mention that because that is another document on which I will rely in due course. He has confirmed that Gary had a history of what he describes as anxiety state and also drug misuse since 1997, and mixed anxiety and depressive disorder in 2001 and he says that he was a known intravenous drug user from about April 2015. That is when he disclosed it to his General Practitioner. He was under the care of the Derbyshire Substance Misuse Service and he's talked about the medication that he was prescribed, and I understand that his last drug screen on the 9th of December was positive for opiates and crack cocaine. He said that Gary had reported starting using heroin, again I am not entirely sure when that was reported, and that there was some talk about trying to move him over to methadone at the next contact. So, there is a little bit more information there from his GP Practice who were clearly involved as were other agencies in Derby in trying to assist and help him. So that is the medical evidence. Now what I would like to do if I can is hear from PC Slee as to the Police Investigation, and I will give you an opportunity of asking some questions. Before I do that, let's just deal with the questions then that you raise which actually PC Slee might have to help me with some of it. I think the first question that you raised in your letter we have probably dealt with, how would the cause of death have affected Gary in his final days and hours. Well you have spoken to your GP that was very helpful, I wouldn't disagree with what the GP was saying, but you know, the reality is we will never really know how unwell he did feel.

Mr Straw. No.

Cor. I suppose we have to assume that he didn't feel so unwell, because he didn't seek any medical attention so I think perhaps he was ignorant to how unwell he had become.

Mr Straw. Yes. Well as I say some of the contradictory factors I mentioned earlier, relevant to that.

Cor. What are they?

Mr Straw. Well, the last time I saw Gary alive was on the Monday, seven days before I found him. The last time I spoke to him was Tuesday. The last time he attended work was Tuesday night, he used to work nights, the last time he attended work was Tuesday night and the last time he attended the pharmacy to pick up his medication was Wednesday.

Cor. Right.

Mr Straw. Now Gary used to pick his medication up religiously, he never missed, or very rarely. To my knowledge he never missed.

Cor. Just tell me what day you found him, I know the date...

Mr Straw.   Monday.

Cor.   So the Wednesday was the last time he was out and about that we know.

Mr Straw.   When I spoke to him on the Tuesday evening, I asked him what he had for his tea, for his meal, and he replied rice snaps, which was a cereal.

Cor.   Oh yes.

Mr Straw.   He loved cereals. There was milk, and there was almost a full box of cereals in the house. So from Tuesday onwards I believe he would have eaten those. What was the other deciding factor… there was another… Yes, there was no outgoing information or activity on his phone after Wednesday, but the contradictory factor was that the neighbour next door said he spoke to him, face to face, from two feet away on the Saturday morning before I found him. And he said, the words was 'are you OK Gary', 'yes fine thanks'.

Cor.   So in your mind you think something happened on the Wednesday.

Mr Straw.   Wednesday or Thursday at the latest. I wonder, I don't know the neighbour, I don't know how reliable he is, and I'm not casting aspersions on his credibility. I wonder whether he got his weekends mixed up or whatever. You see I had started texting Gary at the weekend, we had been in this scenario before with his drugs and everything else and I started texting him on the Saturday and I am sure, with hindsight, that he would have sent me a text

Cor. back because we was very close. So, in my mind it all adds up to sort of Wednesday or Thursday.

Cor. Right.

Mr Straw. But according to the neighbour he saw him walking in the street, spoke to him face to face coming out the door, so there's no mistake in identity, so the only hope, well no hope, is a mistaken day. In my mind, and I know nothing about dead bodies, but to me he looked as though he had been dead longer than sort of Saturday afternoon, say, which could have been the earliest scenario that he would have died if the neighbour did see him.

Cor. Ok. All right. PC Slee, I wonder if you would take the Oath or the Affirmation and perhaps we can start to go through your investigation and we might be able to deal with this issue as well.

PC Slee 14324 upon his Oath states:-

Cor. So was it the East Midlands Ambulance Service who contacted the Police?

Wit. That is correct.

Cor. So what time did the call come through to you on the 18th?

Wit. I got the call at 1519 hours.

Cor. And what information were you given initially?

Wit. We were informed of a sudden death of a male at No 30 Bloomsgrove Road, Ilkeston. The information was passed by EMAS, that the deceased was a known drug user and that his father, David Straw, was also present at the scene. Information was also passed that at the time it was believed the deceased was in a debt to his drug dealer.

Cor. Ok, so Police attended, that included you did it; you were one of the first Police Officers in the scene?

Wit. That is correct.

Cor. And I think your colleague, PC Duffield went with you.

Wit. That's right.

Cor. You spoke to the Paramedics presumably, what if anything did they tell you?

Wit. They initially informed us of the unkempt nature of the property. The fact to be careful of used needles and drug paraphernalia as we entered the property. They informed us where the body was in the property, in an upstairs bedroom on the bed, and also introduced us to David. At the time we met with you.

Mr Straw. Yes.

Wit. Prior to going up to view the body ourselves.

Mr Straw. Yes.

Cor. So you then did go upstairs, did you, and see Gary where he had been found by his father and the Paramedics, of course, had attended to him.

Wit. Yes.

Cor. As far as you were aware he hadn't been moved significantly prior to your arrival.

Wit. No. No, I know I spoke to you and you confirmed that at the time you had seen him but you hadn't moved him and your reactions had been to ring.

Mr Straw. No. I did touch him, and I just hold him briefly but I didn't move him.

Cor. Ok, that's fine. And you could see yourself then the needles and the drug paraphernalia that had already been described to you; you could see that could you?

Wit. That's right, yes.

Cor. Just describe then how it was that you found Gary.

Wit. We found Gary in an upstairs; I believe it was the middle bedroom. He was lying across the bed, knees slightly bent and his feet were hanging off one side of the bed. He was lying on his back I believe, on the bed as we entered the bedroom.

Cor. Any sign of disturbance within the property, or was it difficult to tell because of the unkempt nature?

Wit.   There didn't appear to be any sign of a disturbance and again on speaking to David, you confirmed that on your arrival both the front and rear doors were secure.

Mr Straw.   Well I never checked the rear door, but when the question was raised I said to the Paramedics and they went and tried it. Nobody had been to the back door. They said yes, it's locked, so obviously it would have been locked when I entered.

Wit.   The only slight insecurity was an open window at the front of the property. However, all of the, there were numerous items, on the window ledge itself and also a fair bit of dust and it appeared that no one had entered through that insecurity.

Cor.   Ok. So it looked as if he had died on the bed, on his own, there was no one else in the property, no sign of any third party involvement. He was lying on the bed, presumably it was therefore difficult to tell whether he had collapsed on the bed, but did it look to you as if he had gone to bed and perhaps died whist he was on the bed?

Wit.   It looked like, rather than going to bed, and, you know, because he was lying across it rather than lengthways, it appeared that maybe, I don't know, he had recently slumped onto the bed, or was just having a rest rather than going to bed as such.

Mr Straw.   Well the contributing factor to that as well was, of course, it was the 18th January, the nights was dark and there was no electric lights on in the house whatsoever,

Wit. so he must have passed away or at least felt unwell and lay there while it was still daylight, in my mind anyway.

Cor. Yes.

Wit. I mean I can only compare as to obviously how I would go to bed and that would be to lie lengthways and to get into bed properly rather than lying across the bed.

Mr Straw. Yes.

Wit. So I believe he was either slumped on to it or, like you say, rested during the daytime, or whenever it may have been.

Mr Straw. Well the thing that struck me, I mean, you may say it's not correct, but there was a small amount of urine that was found in his body, and I wonder if he had gone to the bathroom, which was just adjacent, felt unwell, sat on the bed and it all happened, he passed away there and then, but, of course it is all speculation, isn't it.

Cor. It is, but that is of course entirely possible. Anything of note then in terms of your searching of the property, there is nothing else that you found?

Wit. No, we did a search of the body but there was nothing significant during the search.

Cor. You had a Forensic Medical Examiner attend who is of course a doctor employed by the Constabulary, what was Dr Danner's view?

Wit. Dr Danner attended, yes. Dr Danner mentioned that he'd found the deceased, he'd found evidence that the deceased had been injecting into his groin with needles. Dr Danner stated that as a result of this there was a much higher chance of thrombosis the possibility of the subsequent death of Gary.

Cor. So that was his initial view then, it might be to do with that?

Wit. That was his initial view.

Cor. Ok. Was Dr Danner able to give any informal view, and I know that it would have been informal because they are pretty reluctant to commit, aren't they, to paper about how long it was that Gary had been deceased prior to your arrival.

Wit. I don't recall any view given on that.

Cor. What about this neighbour then, what did the neighbour say about the fact that he had seen Gary much more recently?

Wit. So it was myself that took the statement from a Mr Stephen Ingle, who was the direct next door neighbour.

Mr Straw. Yes. I happened to bump into him when I was clearing the house out and, you know, he obviously gave me his apologies and it was himself who sort of gave me the details of how he last saw Gary and when it was. I mean he was most definite that it was then.

Wit. Yes, I mean, when I went to speak to him it's, you know, it's something the Police will do it investigate any sort of crime or unfortunately in this case sudden death. We will always do house to house enquiries to see if anyone has seen or heard anything, and on speaking to Mr Ingle, he was open and stated he didn't really know Gary particularly well, other than being a neighbour to him. He didn't know his name, and simply knew him as his neighbour, and would say hello in passing, but to me he was adamant that he last saw Gary on Saturday 16th January and he said approximately 10:30 in the morning and he said it was simply coincidence that they left their respective properties at the same time and said hello in passing as neighbours would do, and that was it, they went their separate ways.

Mr Straw. I mean the two doors are literally 18 inches apart.

Wit. That's right. They said hello and then went their separate ways and about their daily business.

Mr Straw. Yes.

Cor. So from your enquiries, assuming that Mr Ingle is right with the dates, and I know there is some question about that, that was the last time he was seen alive?

Wit. As far as we're aware, that's the last person.

Cor. Other than Mr Ingle then, let's assume he was confused about the date, who had seen him, who was the last person before that, was it his father?

Wit. You'll have to bear with me, whether it be his father or whether it be his colleagues at work.

Mr Straw. Yes well as I say he did attend there Tuesday evening, I mean Andrea might be able to tell you the Pharmacy; I don't know which one he used.

Unidentified Female. Boots Pharmacy on Bath Street.

Mr Straw. But I know it was the one on Bath Street. But you confirmed that the Pharmacy had said that it was Wednesday, that was the last day.

Cor. So Boots Pharmacy on Bath Street, he picked his prescription up from there on the Wednesday.

Mr Straw. Did he pick his prescription daily or two-daily?

Unidentified Female. I can't remember, that's what I'm trying to think.

Mr Straw. But I know he was, he, you know, he, well I mean records might prove me different but from my experience, he was always very sort of prompt and efficient at picking up his prescription.

Unidentified Female. It was either daily or three times a week because I am kind of thinking in my mind was he due again Friday, and didn't turn up Friday. That what I'm thinking in my head.

Mr Straw. Which I find very strange if he, if he was still up and about, I find it very strange that he didn't pick his medication up.

Cor. So if it was daily he would have gone Thursday, well he would have gone every day up until the Saturday.

Unidentified Female. He would have gone every day, yes, but I don't think was otherwise we would be more kind of confident about that.

Mr Straw.   Yes.

Unidentified Female. I wish I had reflected in my notes now but I am thinking at the time, I was talking to David and saying he should have gone again on the Friday.

Mr Straw.   Yes.

Unidentified Female. And he would have gone, because he was very reliable like clockwork with his collections, so he would have had this Thursday dose at home, if he was, you know, still alive.

Cor.   I mean that does create some difficulties with Mr Ingle's evidence doesn't it PC Slee, and I mean I agree with what you're saying David, that, you know I am not saying I disbelieve what he has said but I do wonder whether he has become confused because everything else seems to point to something catastrophic happening on the Wednesday doesn't it.

Mr Straw.   I mean the cereals may seem insignificant, but I know Gary would have, he used to get through a box of cereals in a day, he used to love his cereals and of course it was quick and easy. He hadn't got to prepare anything, he chucked them in a bowl, poured some milk over and he had got them. So I find it strange that, you know, there was virtually a full box. I mean by his own admission he'd had one meal from them, and it looked as though, to me, that was all that was missing so it didn't appear that any others had been taken which I find strange.

Wit.   As you know, I have spoken with you on the phone...

Mr Straw.   Yes.

Wit.   ...a few times since, and I know that you have raised that point to me, about the evidence of the neighbour, but from, you know, from our point of view...

Mr Straw.   Well, of course, yes, we don't know do we, it can't be proved either way, of course; it is all speculation.

Wit.   That's right.

Cor.   I think that is the problem.

Mr Straw.   Yes.

Cor.   I don't think we are ever going to get to the bottom of that.

Mr Straw.   No, no, well I have accepted that.

Cor.   What I would say to you is this: If you have formed the opinion that something happened on the Wednesday.

Mr Straw.   Yes.

Cor.   Then I don't think you should let the evidence of Mr Ingle persuade you away from that.

Mr Straw.   Well there was also the texts that I sent him as well.

Cor. Well exactly.

Mr Straw. He would of, he would of replied, and with hindsight I ought to have realised that something was strange because he hadn't replied, but I am confident in my own mind that if I'd texted him, you know, I just basically said, you know: are you ok, let me know, you know, just either ring or text to let me know you're Ok, and I texted him three times and that's when I went down.

Cor. Yes.

Mr Straw. And with hindsight I've probably should of heard the alarm bells ringing earlier than I did.

Cor. Hindsight is a wonderful thing.

Mr Straw. Of course, of course. As you said you had been here in the past hadn't you and nothing specific had happened.

Mr Straw. No.

Cor. Anything else PC Slee, as far as your investigation is concerned.

Wit. Nothing really.

Cor. The conclusions of your investigations, of course are consistent with our investigations in terms of the fact that there was nothing suspicious.

Wit. That's right.

Cor. There were no signs of any injuries, I know there was this slight suggestion that he might owe money to somebody and there were some concerns about that, but in terms of his death, nobody else is implicated are they.

Wit. That's right; there was no sign of any third party involvement.

Cor. Ok, all right. And presumably your conclusion therefore is just a tragic accident relating to his drug use.

Wit. That's correct.

Cor. Any questions that you have got for PC Slee that you want to ask him about the investigation that was carried out?

Mr Straw. No, I don't think so; I mean the other question I raised which is again all speculation was that Gary normally left his key in the lock. He used to let himself in, he used to put the key back in the lock and always lock the door. Always, that is something else he did almost religiously because when my Aunt still lived at the property, when she'd been up shopping, very often she returned and if Gary had come in and locked the door, he did it automatic, she couldn't get her own key in the lock so she was, she was hammering on the door of her own house, basically.

Cor. Right.

Mr Straw. But the keys wasn't in the door because that's why when I went in, and I think I've said in my statement to PC Slee, that I assumed he was out at work, or with his friends. But it was yourself I believe that found the keys.

Wit.   That's right.

Mr Straw.   Lying on the floor in front of the settee.

Wit.   They were on the floor just in front of the sofa.

Mr Straw.   But I've made enquiries of his friends and I've done subsequent searches and the spare key that was in the property was still there, so I can't believe why anybody would have had another key cut to let their self in or out if there was a spare key available in the properly, so other than the reason why the key wasn't left in the door. I mean, one of my first conclusions was he had took his own life, and he knew that we would need to get entry. That was me initial thoughts, but obviously it has become clear from the findings that that wasn't the case.

Cor.   I suppose the other explanation is that if he was feeling unwell, that maybe he felt that, you know, he needed ... the same principle might apply.

Mr Straw.   Well possibly, I think it is something that we are never going to be able to find out, isn't it. It's just going to be one of those mysteries that always remain.

Cor.   This is so often the problem at Inquest because I have to say that there are a large proportion of deaths that I deal with where the person dies on their own, there is nobody to witness the death.

Mr Straw.   No.

Cor.   I mean there are exceptions to that, but a lot of people who die in their own home die on their own, and because of that, you know, the Police are at a disadvantage immediately, there are not witnesses, and ultimately at Inquest we are, ourselves. So we do end up doing a lot of this, don't we, a lot of speculating about what might have happened, and I don't think there is any harm in that from your perspective. From my perspective, from a legal perspective, I can only record what I know as facts.

Mr Straw. Of course.

Cor. But from your perspective I don't think there is any harm in that, and going back to this question about, you know, when it was he died, I think you have to rely very heavily on your instincts as a father, and if Wednesday is the day you think it happened, then Wednesday is the day it happened.

Mr Straw. Well, sort of Wednesday or Thursday but you see the Paramedic you stated, I didn't realise this, because I don't know anything about dead bodies, but the Paramedic stated that rigor mortis as present.

Cor. Yes.

Mr Straw. Now again, I don't know any time spans for when that commences or how long it lasts, or whether that would give us a clue.

Cor. It wouldn't really, it's not very specific. All it means is that he didn't die within minutes before you arrived, because the body was cold, and there were changes taking place.

Mr Straw. Yes, yes.

Cor. But beyond that it is not very helpful. But again, there are situations where, you know, Paramedics will, you know, people arrive, find somebody and they are still warm to the touch. We know then that they died only within a few hours beforehand.

Mr Straw. But again, in my statement, I've stated that before I entered the room, I mean the last time I smelt a dead body was my Grandfather in 1958, when he was laid in the front room of the same property, which is what the custom was in those days, he was interred in the front room for a few days before he was buried. And even though I've never smelt a dead body since that 1958, as soon as I started to open the door to enter the room, I got the same unmistakeable smell from all those years ago and it was instantly recognisable to me, which again made me think, well, would that have occurred from Saturday afternoon to Monday? I don't know, I mean it was wintertime, it was cold, and there was no heating on, you know, I checked that, that the heating system hadn't been left on.

Cor. It is difficult, because, you know, changes, people are affected by different things aren't they. It is possible, but I think it is more likely, to be honest with you, that something happened Wednesday or Thursday, from everything that I am being told.

Mr Straw. Yes.

Cor. The only piece of information that doesn't seem to make sense is that from a neighbour.

Mr Straw.   Yes.

Cor.   But I can't make any determinations in that respect.

Mr Straw.   Well I have accepted that that would be the case.

Cor.   Ok, good. Well does that answer all the questions that you ... well, have you had the opportunity of putting all the questions that you have, even if you haven't been able to get a definitive answer from the Police Officer?

Mr Straw.   Yes, I believe so, yes.

Cor.   Ok. Alright. Well I do feel I am in a position to conclude the Inquest. I don't know in the end how helpful this has been to you because, as I just said, I don't know that you have got definitive answers to those questions that you have raised, but at least we have had an opportunity of talking round it haven't; we?

Mr Straw.   Yes.

Cor.   And hopefully hearing from the Police Officer and from me it will have settled things in your mind a little bit. What I have to record now are the facts based on the evidence that I have available to me and I have to answer, if I can, those legal questions that I talked about earlier. So I am going to do that now by going through a Record of Inquest that will be produced in due course in relation to Gary's death. I am going to confirm now that the full name of the deceased will be recorded as Gary David Straw. The medical cause of death, and I rely of course on Dr Hitchcock's report for this is now formally recorded as:

1a   Septic Shock, due to

1b   Multiple Visceral Infarctions and Micro Abscess Formation, due to

1c   Intravenous Drug Abuse

> The answers to the questions 'how', 'when' and 'where' Gary came to his death are answered as follows, that all I can say, based on the evidence that I have available to me is that 'Gary Straw was found deceased at his home on the 18th January 2016'. We have had a lot of discussion in Court here today about when he might have died and based on the evidence I have available to me it remains unclear as to when that happened, but as an aside I reiterate to you again that if you think it was Wednesday or the Thursday, I am certainly not here to persuade you away from that. What I will report though is the date that he was found, rather than the date he died, because that is the only thing that we are sure about.

Mr Straw.   Yes.

Cor.   Now we do know that he had a long documented history if illicit drug abuse. The post mortem toxicology analysis did not reveal acute drug toxicity, but the changes that the Pathologist observed during the course of the post mortem examination, he says were associated with a general pattern of abuse over a number of years, and of course that was supported by the fact that there were recent injection sites noted by the Pathologist in both groins and I think the Doctor who attended, the Police doctor who attended has seen at least one of those. Given all of that evidence it is clear that Gary's death was accidental, but it is formally recorded now that Gary David

Straw died as a result of a drug related death, but it is in the context of the findings that I have just outlined for you. Now I am required to confirm the particulars required by the Births and Deaths Registration Act 1953, and perhaps if I can just check with you David, that the details I have on my file are correct: The first of September 1975 is the date that I have recorded as his birth, and he was born here in Derby.

Mr Straw.   Derby City Hospital, yes.

Cor.   His full name, Gary David Straw.

Mr Straw.   Yes.

Cor.   We know, of course, that he died at his home on the 18th January that was the date he was found. He was a Plumbing and Heating Engineer by occupation.

Mr Straw.   Yes.

Cor.   And his home address was 30, Bloomsgrove Road, Ilkeston in Derbyshire.

Mr Straw.   Yes.

Cor.   Those details then will be passed on to the Registrar. It will be the Registrar in Chesterfield that deals with the registration of Gary's death, but the good news is that you won't need to attend. I will organise for registration of his death for you so the onus isn't on you to register, I will do that, and what we will do is we will pass on your details, I see I have got both your mobile telephone number and your home telephone number, to the Registrar and they will give you a ring probably towards the middle of next week. By then they will have registered his death, it will all be done, but they will phone you to ask you whether or not you want a copy of the certificate, and if you do, how many. They will simply put them in the post to you and you will receive those in due course.

Mr Straw.   Ok.

Cor.   Now when you get the death certificate you will see recorded on there, amongst other things, the medical cause of death which is formalised today, together with my formal finding that he died as a result of drug related death. The broader findings that I have outlined to you won't be included on the death certificate, but they are recorded on the Record of Inquest which is the final document that remains here on our file. If you decide you want a copy of that, you won't need to produce that for anybody but if you do what a copy of that, if you let us know we can send you a copy of that as well, but that is the only public document that is produced following an Inquest.

Mr Straw.   And what's that document again?

Cor.   That is called the Record of Inquest.

Mr Straw.   Right.

Cor.   That is the document that I produce, and that will remain, as I say, on file. It is not published anywhere but it is a public document so if anybody, including you, wants a copy of that, you are entitled to it.

Mr Straw.   Ok.

Cor.   So do let us know if you want it. As far as I am concerned then, the investigation is completed. Can I thank PC Slee for his investigation and for the evidence that he has given here today, extremely helpful to me. I have to say that the enquiries that you've made have obviously been very thorough as well as it struck me during the course of this Inquest that if you decided you wanted to go back to working, I think being a Police Officer probably is a profession that would suit you very well, because I think you have done extremely well and I know part of if of course is the desire to understand how your son died.

Mr Straw.   Yes, of course.

Cor.   But I have rarely had a family member in Court that has been so thorough in their own investigations, and it has been very helpful to me as well, and I hope that it has helped you through the very long grieving process that I am sure you are now... er, feeling... although I am hoping that now that the Inquest is over, you can now move onto the next stage of all that.

Mr Straw.   Yes.

Cor.   Can I thank both of you for coming today, it has been an absolute pleasure having you in Court; it is nice to see the family supported in this particular environment. He was obviously very well supported by everybody involved, just a terrible shame of course that he succumbed in the end, ultimately to his drug addiction, which of course was very damaging to him, both mentally and also as it turned out physically as well.

Mr Straw. Yes, yes.

Cor. Can I offer you my condolences.

Mr Straw. Thank you.

Cor. It has been lovely to meet you, I am sorry it is in such difficult circumstances. If there is anything else we can do, you know where PC Slee is, but also do feel free to come to us, as well.

Mr Straw. Can I equally thank you in turn for your time and obviously professionalism today.

Cor. Thank you. Thank you all. Right, any more questions or are you all content?

Mr Straw. No, no.

Unidentified Female. Where does Dave apply for this report?

Cor. If you just give us a ring, or let us know in writing, we will just send you a copy. It won't be completed... hopefully it will be done if not today then tomorrow, so by tomorrow it should be available. Just give us a ring and we will send one through the post to you.

Mr Straw. Thank you very much.

Cor. But it just reflects what I have just explained to you, basically.

Mr Straw.　　Yes, ok.

Conclusion: Drug-related Death

As far as we are aware we only have one life

But as we live our life in reality

Do we not live another for our hopes?

So perhaps we have two lives,

One for reality and one for our hopes.

David Michael Straw

CHAPTER 17

Time moved on as it always does, nothing eventful happening, the days passing by routinely. The sale of the house was in the hands of the new estate agents and almost immediately I received an offer, slightly less that I realistically wanted, so a compromise was made, and I accepted a figure in the middle of what they wanted and what I thought was reasonable. The sale was on and I hoped it would all go through without a hitch. Mixed feelings yet again, glad for it to be sold but obviously a little sad it was no longer in the family after all those years. The contracts were signed and a date was given for the handover.

In the afternoon of the last day of my ownership I went to the house. I slipped Gary's keys into the lock and let myself in for the very last time. It was only bricks and mortar, as they say. I knew that, of course, but that house had played such a big part in my life, my mum's and my grandparents' life as well. I wandered round the empty rooms, my old bedroom, my mum's old bedroom; that was the room in which I had found Gary on that fateful day. it seemed a lifetime ago.

When I was undergoing counselling my therapist asked me if I suffered flashbacks to the time I had found Gary. I told her I didn't really know the definition of a flashback, but if it was being able to close my eyes and relive every moment in a vivid detail then the answer was yes.

As I stood there in the spot where Gary had died I closed my eyes and it was all there, all happening again, just like watching a video replay. I moved on, walked round all the empty rooms, eventually sitting down at the bottom of the stairs. I closed my eyes and suddenly the house was full of ghosts, my mum, my aunt, my grandparents, all my relatives and, of course, Gary. All of them now passed away, all of them here in the house with me. I saw myself as a child, I saw myself growing up to be a young man. I saw so many things, none of them real, of course, just memories, so many memories, but they seemed so real and it saddened me because it was in the past; all my loved ones around me were in the past.

I wanted to revisit those times, spend time with all those people who had meant so much to me but, of course, it was impossible; they and those times had gone, never to return. All that was left was the future.

I loved my wife and always wanted to be with her, but I knew my future would always have something missing. The family I had grown up with were all gone, I had no brothers or sisters, no children. Even with lots of people around you every day you can still feel lonely. And as I sat there I had never felt so alone in all my life. All the connections with my past had gone, all I had left were memories. I opened my eyes and I returned to the real world. I got up, walked out of the house, locking the door behind me for the final time, and walked away. I didn't look back.

As I had grown older I had taken it for granted that all my older relatives were dying. It was sad, of course it was, but it was normal, it was what happened and I just accepted it without question. Only when I lost Gary did I realise that I had no one from my close family left around me. Only then did it really hit me.

Christmas was drawing ever nearer. It was a time I had always loved, and my Christmas periods as a child had, to me, been truly magical. The Christmas periods I had spent with Gary had been magical. As you grow older, Christmas, although a lovely time of year, seems to lose the magic, especially if there are no children to enjoy it with. This Christmas certainly wasn't going to be magical; I was dreading it. Christmas is a time for families and I knew I was going to miss Gary even more. It was going to be difficult for my wife as well. We had lost Elizabeth's father a few months earlier and he would be sadly missed. Christmas came and went, not quite as bad as I envisaged but none the less as I had predicted; it certainly wasn't magical.

Dot paid me her last visit over this period and it was time for her to move on. She obviously had new casualties of life to deal with. I was sorry to say goodbye for I had found her visits and her input a great comfort to me, but I accepted that I was also moving on, moving forward. Things were becoming a little clearer. The pain and despair I had felt in those first months after Gary had died were slowly starting to lose their grip. The stomach-wrenching pain was turning slowly into a dull remorseless ache. It wasn't sharp like someone sticking a knife into you and twisting it any more. I knew I would always hurt but it was slowly lessening with time.

The anniversary of Gary's death and his funeral came and went. They weren't too painful surprisingly, just dates on a calendar. What I did find significant was that when the anniversary of his death passed I wasn't experiencing events for the first time without Gary. The first snowdrops and daffodils of spring, Easter time, my first cat-fishing trip, all of these seemed a little bit easier the second time around. I had been wandering around in a fog of despair, but slowly it was beginning to clear, the first feeble rays of sunlight slowly clearing the mist, opening up clearings so you could begin to see your way forward once more. Of course there were times when it thickened and, once again, I was enveloped and lost but, slowly and surely, it was beginning to clear and slowly brighten.

Perhaps I did not tell you

How much I really cared.

I tell you now so many times.

I pray those words are heard.

David Michael Straw

CHAPTER 18

My story with Gary is nearly over, my journey through life with him obviously finished, although he will continue to influence me until I die. My life since Gary's death has been horrendous, a living nightmare, but somehow you find the resources to cope and you find the strength to see you through. Someone once said to me, 'I don't know how you coped. I know I wouldn't have'.

I told him, 'Yes, you would, because you have to. You have no choice.'

My life is slowly coming together; it has to, otherwise the evil of drugs will have gained another victim. My hatred of all social drugs is strong and passionate. You may say it is self-inflicted, that no one forces them to indulge, but if you have no sympathy for the drug-takers themselves, spare a thought for their families, forced to stand helplessly by and watch them destroy themselves. I have always felt I carried much of the blame for Gary's demise, but I also know the only person who can save them from ultimate destruction is themselves.

My own life since Gary's death, whilst awful, has taught me many things; unfortunately mostly too late to influence my own dilemma. It has changed me for ever. I believe it has possibly made me a better person, it has certainly given me the compassion to appreciate other people's suffering. If I see a family now that loses a son or daughter, especially if that loss is sudden or unexpected, I can feel their grief, their loss. I know exactly what they are having to endure. Unless you have experienced that loss yourself you cannot begin to comprehend the misery and upset. You may imagine you can, but I would say it is impossible to fully understand unless you have lived through the ordeal.

Writing this story has helped me immensely; putting my innermost thoughts and emotions down on paper have been an outpouring of my grief. Whether any one will want to read my story is possibly unimportant. I say possibly, because if it can help anyone to fight the evil of drugs, even in a small way, then that can only be for the good.

My life has been changed forever, by heroin in particular. I personally have never been tempted to use drugs, nor will I ever want to. Millions of people do, and these drugs must have a power beyond my comprehension. They know they are being destroyed and that they are also destroying the lives of their loved ones, but they seem powerless to alter their actions. My own son, Gary, once told me he was ashamed of the things he had done to obtain his fix, but when your desire for heroin was so strong it didn't matter to you; it was of no consequence what your actions were, the only thing important to you was to score.

It seems unreasonable to a none-drug-taking individual, but a lot of the people who take drugs are not bad people, just people who, perhaps for whatever reason, do not like their own personal little world in which they live. It was once described to me by someone, that after taking heroin all your worries and anxieties were replaced with a feeling of utter contentment, like wrapping a warm blanket around you and shutting out, if only for a little while, all the worries of the world. I for one, and perhaps yourself, should consider that we have been lucky enough not to feel that desolate. I am certainly not condoning the use of drugs, far from it, they are evil but we should remember not everyone can take the stresses of life unaided.

Perhaps I have over simplified the reasons for taking drugs. It is a far too complex question for me to understand. The one thing I do know is that they have robbed me of the most precious thing in my entire life, my son, and all I do is try to make some sense of it. I try but I always fail.

Why did you leave, where did you go?

We never said goodbye.

Why you left I do not know.

Can someone tell me why?

David Michael Straw

The following lines of this poem (for want of a better description) I have written myself. I have no personal experience of taking heroin or indeed any other drug for that matter, but from the conversations I have had with my own son and other drug users, I am fairly certain it is a true, if not simplified, description of the way of life and death that using Heroin will bring.

I have written it blessed with hindsight after the tragic death of my much loved son, Gary. I was told by my son several years ago that the term 'to ride the white horse' is an analogy used to describe the taking of Heroin.

The poem itself was written very quickly, in roughly fifteen to twenty minutes, I suppose. It was as if the poem was writing itself, the other possibility, of course, is that someone was writing it for me.

RIDE THE WHITE HORSE

'Ride the white horse,' isn't that what they say?

But to sit in the saddle, a price you must pay.

At first it will amaze you, you will dream of my power.

I will be there to seduce you, no matter the hour.

I will comfort you and hold you so safe in my arms,

You will wonder from where do I get my subliminal charms.

You will tingle and tremble at the thrill that I give,

And without me you will feel your life you can't live.

Before too long your love will turn slowly to hate,

You won't be able to leave me; your need will be great.

You will try to desert me, I will drive you insane,

Not content to inhale me, you will drive me deep in your vein.

Your life will be ruined; it all turns to dust,

You know you can't leave me but you feel that you must.

To cheat and to steal, there won't be a care.

Just so long as I am near; I have to be there.

I will start to destroy you; it goes on till the end.

You will try to forsake me but your ways you can't mend.

You desire me, you want me, I am all that you crave.

I will always be with you as you go to your grave.

David Michael Straw 2016

CHAPTER 19

The second Christmas without Gary is almost with us, it is unbelievably nearly two years since his death. How do I feel now after the passing of time? Some of the things I am going to say I realise I have spoken of before, but I make no apologies for reiterating myself because these thoughts are important to me and are uppermost in my mind.

It has taken me all this time to finally write what will be the last chapter in my story. Some of my writing has flowed profusely, almost as profusely as the tears that flowed after Gary's death. At other times I have found it difficult to put pen to paper and commit my innermost thoughts. It was almost as if I would be committing my thoughts to immortality which, in a way, I suppose I am. However, I have reached this point in my life and I repeat the question, How do I feel now? In all honesty, not a great deal different to how I felt almost two years ago. Yes, I have learnt to cope and the bitter rawness of it all has subsided, and I know I can find a way forward and still have a life worth living.

I still miss Gary, of course, and in fact I think I miss him more now than I did initially. I think of him each and every day. I actually think of him many times each day and I find myself wondering how all these thoughts and feelings and the whole experience may manifest themselves in the future.

I spoke in my tribute to Gary at his funeral and I quote, 'For me there is no sunlit meadow, no chorus of birdsong, no butterflies flitting from flower to flower, indeed the place in which I find myself is so deep and so dark I fear I may never walk in these places again'. Well, I have walked in these places again and hopefully I will continue to walk in them, but the sky is not so blue, the grass so green, nor the birdsong so sweet and I know they never can be.

It is obvious that things have affected me badly and Gary's death has hit me harder than I would ever have thought possible, but there is no way of altering the facts or indeed the way I feel. I have tried to be angry with Gary for what he has put me through, to alienate my thoughts towards him, after all he chose the path he walked down, but I simply cannot do it. What causes someone to live their life in this way? Why do they feel the need to ride the white horse so strongly? Even with my experience with drugs I cannot give you an answer, other than to say their power is far beyond my comprehension.

If I had the chance to do it all again what would I do differently? In all honesty I don't know. Would I have zero tolerance from the very beginning and, if so, would it have made any difference? If I had thrown Gary out at the first signs of drugs, told him not to contact me again until he was totally free of them, would it have averted disaster or would that disaster have arrived even sooner? There is no way of knowing, but what I do know is that it would take someone far stronger than myself to have achieved it.

You worry about them when you know what they are doing, but you worry even more when you don't know for, if you lose contact with them anything could be happening. They could be all alone and badly in need of help. How could you live with yourself if you let that happen? There is just no easy answer.

What is so compelling in riding that white horse that they ride it all the way to oblivion? Gary took that ride and once he was astride he found he couldn't stop and dismount; it was a ride to his death. Gary rode the white horse and he certainly lived in its shadow, as did I.

If you chose to take these drugs you ride into a world of pain and anguish and not only do you go there yourselves, but you take all of your loved ones along with you for that ride into hell.

I close my eyes and see your face,

I hear your voice so clear.

The tears that fall do not disgrace

The memories held so dear.

David Michael Straw

The following poems were written as entirely separate entities.

Only when I had finished writing the 'Darkening' which was the latter of the two to be written did I realise that both of the poems combined well with each other.

For that reason I have placed both poems together in this book.

Neither poem has anything directly connected to my son or his death.

I include them in my book however because if it was not for the death of my son or the emotional changes it caused within myself they would certainly never have been written. They are also reminiscent of the many hours Gary and I spent together experiencing the night and it various moods and of course the dawn, a seemingly new beginning, everything appearing fresh and renewed.

THE DARKENING

The sun sinks slowly through the sky

With no excuse it takes its leave

Its heavenly light begins to die

Twilight gives a short reprieve.

The gloaming turns to dark so deep

Distance hidden from our sight

Perhaps a time for most to sleep

To seek the sanctuary of the night.

Creatures of the hour arise

Under a darkened shroud, it is their world

A chorus of their ghostly cries

Imaginations left unfurled.

The moon appears a glowing sphere

Rising with majestic grace

Its presence lending atmosphere

The eerie light not out of place.

For millennia it has shone its light

Countless acts it watched unfold

An object of mystery shining bright

Its secrets never to be told.

Elemental forces seem to thrive

Unyielding shadows feed our fears

Supernatural thoughts become alive

A childish dread awoken despite our years.

Impatiently we await the dawn

A night of overly long duration

The morning arrives the spirit reborn

Imagined horrors turning to elation.

D M STRAW 2018

MORNING LIGHT

Morning dawns the horizon bright
A blood red orb ascends the sky
It turns the darkness into light
Night is over and day is nigh

Birds of the air they now awake
Filling the dawn with wondrous song
No orchestra could such music make
Their singing loud, their melodies long

A cobalt sky with colours smeared
Shades of gold that clothe the ground
Wraiths of mist, now disappeared
Dew shining like diamonds all around

The sun turned golden now gaining height
Its battle won, the darkness banished
A vista of blue with clouds of white
Conceding defeat the moon has vanished

The morning has arrived the world renewed

All colours bright and freshly painted

It's difficult to deny its joyous mood

The day begins, as yet untainted

It is my favourite time I must confess

Nature wears the morning like a crown

Without a doubt her finest dress

For me by far her prettiest gown

David Michael Straw

A day off from fishing in Cornwall

Catfishing in Spain

Catfishing in France

Catfishing in France

Carp fishing in England

CHAPTER 20

I shared countless hours with Gary when he was a boy and a man. Any time spent with your son can only be special but, of all those hours, the most special to my son and myself have to be the ones we spent fishing together. We shared a common interest which bonded us together. Sometimes we fished for a few hours, other times we would spend up to a fortnight, camped on the banks of some lake or river. We fished all over England and also abroad in France and Spain.

We had so many other destinations and adventures planned for the future. Dreams which will now never materialise. Our fishing trips were not so much a pastime but more of a way of life. All those wonderful times we spent together.

Those early dawns; the sunlight slanting through the mist as it rose wraith-like from the surface of the water; the singing of the birds, the call of the cuckoo in spring; the fragrance of the flowers and the tree blossom in their season; those moonlight nights, the clouds scudding across the sky, the moon obscured, turning the night into intense darkness, only to reappear again and flood everywhere once more with its eerie light; the calling of the owls as they flitted back and forth across the darkened meadows; the distant barking of a fox; the lateness of the hour giving it a feeling of loneliness and isolation.

So many memories, so many golden times we shared together. I still experience these things, but I experience them alone. Gary is not with me to share them. They are still magical but they can never be the same. How could they be? But the memories they evoke will last a lifetime and perhaps beyond.

No matter where you go,

No matter how long it takes,

One day I will find you,

In a place we know from dreams.

Hetty's

Hetty's Charity was founded in 1996 by a group of mums who had their lives turned upside down by a loved one's drug misuse. Today, Hetty's charity delivers emotional and practical support/ advice to families affected by drug or alcohol misuse across the 7 districts of Nottinghamshire, supporting over 250 families every single month.

Families are at the centre of everything that Hetty's do. We know that each family has a unique, dynamic structure, and we work with each individual family being affected by a family member's substance misuse to ensure that they are given the appropriate support at the appropriate time.

Unfortunately, we do not have a magic wand and we acknowledge that for the families and the substance misuser the journey is often long and extremely hard, with many turbulent times along the way. But you do not have to cope alone, Hetty's team of staff and volunteers are here to offer a listening ear, and support you throughout the process.

Hetty's provide a variety of services and psychosocial interventions to help families recover, including;

- Telephone Helpline 9am-7pm 365 days a year
- Face to face support
- Family Mediation
- Kinships Care (to extended family members who have taken on fulltime care and parental responsibility to children who can no longer live with birth parents due to parental substance misuse.)
- Complementary Therapies
- Peer Support Groups
- Educational and awareness training workshops
- Volunteering and Fundraising Opportunities

If you are struggling, live in Nottinghamshire and need support, then please contact us on: -
0800 0850 941 · info@hettys.org.uk · Facebook @Hettys2013